COMMAND SUMMARY (cont

Pull-down menu/ selection	Command menu/ selection		
Volume/			
Log disk	Std/Log or Log disk	L	Dir/File
Log options	Alt/Log disk	Alt-L	Dir/File
Release	Alt/Release disk	Alt-R	Dir/File
Next disk	Std/< or >	< or >	Dir/File
Switch to disk	Ctrl/Log disk	Ctrl-L	Dir/File
Available space	Std/Avail	A	Dir
Format diskette	Alt/format	Alt-F2	Dir/File
Name	Std/Volume	V	Dir
Print	Std/Print	P	Dir
Statistics	Std/stats	?	Dir/File
Wash deleted space	Alt/Wash disk	Alt-W	Dir
Tagged/			
Attributes	Ctrl/Attributes	Ctrl-A	File
Batch	Ctrl/Batch	Ctrl-B	File
Copy files	Ctrl/Copy	Ctrl-C	File
Copy with paths	Alt/Copy	Alt-C	File
Delete	Ctrl/Delete	Ctrl-D	File
Move files	Ctrl/Move	Ctrl-M	File
Move with paths	Alt/Move	Alt-M	File
New date	Ctrl/New date	Ctrl-N	File
Print	Ctrl/Print	Ctrl-P	File
Rename	Ctrl/Rename	Ctrl-R	File
Search	Ctrl/Search	Ctrl-S	File
View	Ctrl/View	Ctrl-V	File
Zip and Arc	Ctrl/archive files	Ctrl-F5	File
Tag/			
Directory files	Std/Tag	T	Dir
All disk files	Ctrl/Tag	Ctrl-T	Dir
All by attributes	Alt/Tag	Alt-T	Dir/File
untag/Directory files	Std/Untag	U	Dir
untag/All disk files	Ctrl/Untag	Ctrl-U	Dir

Up & Running Series from SYBEX

Look for Up & Running books on a variety of popular software topics. Current titles include:

Up & Running with **AutoSketch 3**
Up & Running with **Carbon Copy Plus**
Up & Running with **DOS 3.3**
Up & Running with **Flight Simulator**
Up & Running with **Harvard Graphics**
Up & Running with **Lotus 1-2-3 Release 2.2**
Up & Running with **Lotus 1-2-3 Release 3.1**
Up & Running with **Norton Utilities**
Up & Running with **Norton Utilities 5**
Up & Running with **PageMaker 4 on the PC**
Up & Running with **PageMaker on the Macintosh**
Up & Running with **PC Tools Deluxe 6**
Up & Running with **PC-Write**
Up & Running with **PROCOMM PLUS**
Up & Running with **Q & A**
Up & Running with **Quattro Pro 3**
Up & Running with **Quicken 4**
Up & Running with **ToolBook for Windows**
Up & Running with **Turbo Pascal 5.5**
Up & Running with **Windows 3.0**
Up & Running with **Windows 286/386**
Up & Running with **WordPerfect 5.1**
Up & Running with **WordPerfect Library/Office PC**
Up & Running with **Your Hard Disk**

Computer users are not all alike.
Neither are SYBEX books.

We know our customers have a variety of needs. They've told us so. And because we've listened, we've developed several distinct types of books to meet the needs of each of our customers. What are you looking for in computer help?

If you're looking for the basics, try the **ABC's** series. You'll find short, unintimidating tutorials and helpful illustrations. For a more visual approach, select **Teach Yourself**, featuring screen-by-screen illustrations of how to use your latest software purchase.

Mastering and **Understanding** titles offer you a step-by-step introduction, plus an in-depth examination of intermediate-level features, to use as you progress.

Our **Up & Running** series is designed for computer-literate consumers who want a no-nonsense overview of new programs. Just 20 basic lessons, and you're on your way.

We also publish two types of reference books. Our **Instant References** provide quick access to each of a program's commands and functions. SYBEX **Encyclopedias** provide a *comprehensive reference* and explanation of all of the commands, features and functions of the subject software.

Sometimes a subject requires a special treatment that our standard series doesn't provide. So you'll find we have titles like **Advanced Techniques, Handbooks, Tips & Tricks**, and others that are specifically tailored to satisfy a unique need.

We carefully select our authors for their in-depth understanding of the software they're writing about, as well as their ability to write clearly and communicate effectively. Each manuscript is thoroughly reviewed by our technical staff to ensure its complete accuracy. Our production department makes sure it's easy to use. All of this adds up to the highest quality books available, consistently appearing on best seller charts worldwide.

You'll find SYBEX publishes a variety of books on every popular software package. Looking for computer help? Help Yourself to SYBEX.

For a complete catalog of our publications:

SYBEX Inc.
2021 Challenger Drive, Alameda, CA 94501
Tel: (415) 523-8233/(800) 227-2346 Telex: 336311
Fax: (415) 523-2373

Up & Running with XTreeGold™ 2

Robin Merrin

San Francisco • Paris • Düsseldorf • Soest

Acquisitions Editor: David Clark
Series Editor: Joanne Cuthbertson
Copy Editor: Jim Miller
Project Editor: Brendan Fletcher
Technical Editor: Jon Forrest
Word Processors: Scott Campbell, Lisa Mitchell
Book Designer: Elke Hermanowski
Icon Designer: Helen Bruno
Screen Graphics: Cuong Le
Desktop Production Artist: Helen Bruno
Proofreader: Barbara Dahl
Indexer: Ted Laux
Cover Designer: Archer Design

SYBEX is a registered trademark of SYBEX, Inc.

TRADEMARKS: SYBEX has attempted throughout this book to distinguish proprietary trademarks from descriptive terms by following the capitalization style used by the manufacturer.

SYBEX is not affiliated with any manufacturer.

Every effort has been made to supply complete and accurate information. However, SYBEX assumes no responsibility for its use, nor for any infringement of the intellectual property rights of third parties which would result from such use.

Copyright ©1991 SYBEX Inc., 2021 Challenger Drive, Alameda, CA 94501. World rights reserved. No part of this publication may be stored in a retrieval system, transmitted, or reproduced in any way, including but not limited to photocopy, photograph, magnetic or other record, without the prior agreement and written permission of the publisher.

Library of Congress Card Number: 91-65166
ISBN: 0-89588-820-3

Manufactured in the United States of America
10 9 8 7 6 5 4 3 2 1

SYBEX
Up & Running Books

The Up & Running series of books from SYBEX has been developed for committed, eager PC users who would like to become familiar with a wide variety of programs and operations as quickly as possible. We assume that you are comfortable with your PC and that you know the basic functions of word processing, spreadsheets, and database management. With this background, Up & Running books will show you in 20 steps what particular products can do and how to use them.

Who this book is for

Up & Running books are designed to save you time and money. First, you can avoid purchase mistakes by previewing products before you buy them—exploring their features, strengths, and limitations. Second, once you decide to purchase a product, you can learn its basics quickly by following the 20 steps—even if you are a beginner.

What this book provides

The first step usually covers software installation in relation to hardware requirements. You'll learn whether the program can operate with your available hardware as well as various methods for starting the program. The second step often introduces the program's user interface. The remaining 18 steps demonstrate the program's basic functions, using examples and short descriptions.

Contents and structure

A clock shows the amount of time you can expect to spend at your computer for each step. Naturally, you'll need much less time if you only read through the step rather than complete it at your computer.

Special symbols and notes

You can also focus on particular points by scanning the short notes in the margins and locating the sections you are most interested in.

In addition, three symbols highlight particular sections of text:

The Action symbol highlights important steps that you will carry out.

The Tip symbol indicates a practical hint or special technique.

The Warning symbol alerts you to a potential problem and suggestions for avoiding it.

We have structured the Up & Running books so that the busy user spends little time studying documentation and is not burdened with unnecessary text. An Up & Running book cannot, of course, replace a lengthier book that contains advanced applications. However, you will get the information you need to put the program to practical use and to learn its basic functions in the shortest possible time.

We welcome your comments

SYBEX is very interested in your reactions to the Up & Running series. Your opinions and suggestions will help all of our readers, including yourself. Please send your comments to: SYBEX Editorial Department, 2021 Challenger Drive, Alameda, CA 94501.

Preface

Since the development of the first XTree program in 1983, XTree, XTreePro, and XTreePro Gold have been among the most popular and highly regarded utility programs on the market. With each new release, users have found their capabilities as file managers extended to new areas, including sophisticated disk management, information management, and even application management. Now, XTreeGold 2.0 uses pull-down menus to help first-time users get up to speed quickly and learn the more sophisticated features without too much difficulty.

While XTree Company was making it easier for novice users, they were not neglecting power users. If you rely on XTreeGold to manage large hard disks, or if you are responsible for all your organization's PCs, you will find that the new logging capabilities, undelete feature, Alt Move command, and XTreeMenu for application management are worth the price of upgrading.

Up & Running with XTreeGold 2 covers all the basics in XTreePro Gold 1.0 and XTreeGold 2.0, as well as most of the advanced capabilities. In 20 timed steps, you will learn how to use XTreeGold to get your work done quickly. And that's exactly what you want from a utility program.

Table of Contents

Step 1	Installing XTreeGold	1
Step 2	The User Interface	7
Step 3	File Selection Techniques	17
Step 4	Disk and Directory Selection	25
Step 5	Customizing the Tree Display	31
Step 6	Copying and Backing Up	37
Step 7	Deleting Items	45
Step 8	Moving Items	53
Step 9	Renaming Items	61
Step 10	Browsing Directories	65
Step 11	Viewing Files	71
Step 12	Searching through Files	79
Step 13	The Application Menu	83
Step 14	Launching Applications	91
Step 15	Archiving Files	95
Step 16	Extracting Archived Files	101
Step 17	Comparing Files	107
Step 18	Undeleting Files	115
Step 19	Editing Files	119
Step 20	Customizing XTreeGold	129

Step 1
Installing XTreeGold

XTreeGold requires the following to run:

- A minimum of 256 Kb of RAM
- A minimum of 722,000 bytes of hard disk space
- DOS 3.1 or greater
- 100% IBM-PC compatibility

XTreeGold does not require a mouse, but if you are a mouse user you can take advantage of some nice mouse shortcuts.

Both XTreeGold 1.0 and 2.0 include four 5¼" and two 3½" disks for installation. Step 1 tells you how to install and start XTreeGold from these disks.

The Installation Menu

The installation process is driven by the INSTALL program and by items you select from the Installation Menu.

To begin the installation process, first insert disk #1 in disk drive A or B and then:

1. Type **A:** or **B:** (type the letter of the drive you'll be installing from) and press Enter.
2. Type **INSTALL** and press Enter.

The installation menu shown in Figure 1.1 appears, with the *IN-FORMATION* option highlighted and default values showing for the disk drive, directory, and batch file options to be used in installing XTreeGold. To select an option on the menu, press the Up and Down Arrows or Tab to move to the option, and then press Enter. Your mouse will not operate until you have installed XTreeGold.

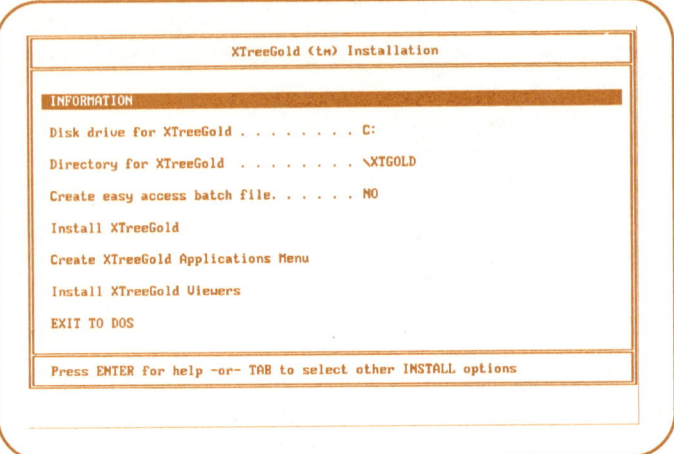

Figure 1.1: The XTreeGold 2.0 installation menu

The three options available from this menu are:

- Installing XTreeGold with or without a batch file.
- Creating an application menu that lists and organizes the programs XTreeGold finds on your hard disk(s).
- Installing one or more of the available file viewers.

XTreePro Gold 1.0 does not include the second or third options.

You must install XTreeGold before you create a menu or install viewers.

Installing XTreeGold

You can install XTreeGold quickly from the installation menu by using the defaults displayed there. Simply move the highlight bar to Install XTreeGold and press Enter. Or change any or all of the defaults using the following steps.

Installing XTreeGold 3

To install XTreeGold on a disk drive and directory other than the defaults:

1. Press the Down Arrow or Tab to highlight *Disk drive for XTreeGold,* then press Enter.
2. Type the letter of any valid disk drive.
3. Press the Down Arrow or Tab to highlight *Directory for XTreeGold,* then press Enter.
4. Type the name of any valid path, using backslashes between directory names. For example, type **\xtree\gold2**. Press Enter.

To create an easy access batch file, press the Down Arrow or Tab to highlight *Create easy access batch file,* then press Enter.

To install using the changes you've made on the menu, press the Down Arrow or Tab to highlight *Install XTreeGold,* and then press Enter.

The installation process begins. If you are installing from 5¼" disks, XTreeGold prompts you to insert disk #2 when it's needed.

If XTreeGold detects a previous XTree version, it prompts for confirmation that you want to install the new version. Continue or cancel the installation.

As you continue with the installation, you will see words like *copying, searching, exploding,* and *extracting* on the screen. XTreeGold is unarchiving all the files it needs to install properly. Once the process is complete, the installation menu appears again. Select *EXIT TO DOS* from the menu or continue the installation process.

Creating an Application Menu

The application menu capabilities of XTreeGold 2.0 are significantly improved over version 1.0. The XTreeGold 2.0 Application

The XTreeGold Application Scanner

Scanner reads your hard disks for the more than 800 applications that it recognizes. It then creates an organized application menu containing the applications it has found. Step 13 covers application menu capabilities.

If you want XTreeGold to create a menu for you now:

1. Press the Down Arrow or Tab to highlight *Create XTreeGold Application Menu,* and press Enter.
2. When the menu has been completed, the message *Press any key* appears at the bottom of the screen. Press any key to return to the menu.

You can display the menu as soon as you have started XTreeGold. Select *EXIT TO DOS* from the menu or continue the installation process.

Selecting Viewers

XTree-Gold 2.0 viewers

XTreeGold viewers enable you to display the contents of files created with many popular applications. XTreeGold 2.0 has many more viewers than version 1.0. In version 1.0, the viewers are installed automatically. Version 2.0 gives you the choice of installing all viewers, selected viewers, or no viewers.

To install all the viewers, you need an additional 714,000 bytes of free disk space. Expect to use between 18,000 and 85,000 bytes of disk space for each viewer you select. Most viewers require between 20,000 and 30,000 bytes.

To install all the viewers:

1. Press the Down Arrow or Tab to highlight *Install XTreeGold Viewers,* and press Enter.
2. The viewer list appears with *INSTALL ALL VIEWERS* highlighted. Press Enter to install all the viewers.
3. Insert the disk(s) XTreeGold asks for and press Enter. XTreeGold automatically returns to the menu.

Installing XTreeGold 5

To install a selection of viewers:

1. Press the Down Arrow or Tab to highlight *Install XTreeGold Viewers,* and press Enter.
2. Press any Arrow key or Tab to highlight a viewer in the list on the screen, and press Enter.
3. Insert the disk XTreeGold asks for, and press Enter.
4. For each additional viewer that you want to install, highlight your choice on the screen and press Enter.
5. When you are finished, highlight *Return to INSTALL program,* on the bottom left of the screen, and press Enter.

This completes the installation process. Now select EXIT TO DOS from the menu, and, when the prompt appears, type Y to confirm.

Starting XTreeGold

There are two basic methods for starting XTreeGold. If you have installed XTreeGold without creating an easy access batch file (you selected *No* for the third option on the installation menu), proceed as follows:

1. Type **cd\xtgold** and press Enter.
2. Type **xtgold** and press Enter.

If you have installed XTreeGold with an easy access batch file (you selected *Yes* for the third option on the installation menu), just type **xtgold** and press Enter.

When XTreeGold starts, the main display appears. Step 2 will show you where to go from here.

Starting XTreeGold with a batch file

Quitting XTreeGold

To quit XTreeGold whenever the Quit command is displayed on the command menu at the bottom of the screen, use one of the following methods to select the Quit command from the Command menu or the XTree pull-down menu:

- Press Q.
- Click the left mouse button on *Quit* in the command menu at the lower right of the screen.

If *Quit* is not displayed on the bottom of the screen, press Esc until you see it.

If you are using version 2.0, you can also use the following methods to quit:

- Open the XTree pull-down menu by clicking the left mouse button in the upper left corner of the screen; then click *Quit XTreeGold*.
- Open the XTree pull-down menu by pressing F10. When the menu bar appears, you may have to press the Left or Right Arrow to open the XTree pull-down menu. Press Q.

Step 2 explains more about using the command menus and pull-down menus.

Step 2

The User Interface

When you start XTreeGold, the first thing you see is the main display, shown in Figure 2.1. The main display includes three key elements: windows that list files or display a directory tree; boxes that display information about the disks, directories, and files you are working with; and access to the menus containing commands. Step 2 describes these elements and how to use them.

Figure 2.1: XTreeGold's main display

Directory and File Windows

The Directory window contains a directory tree. This directory tree is a diagram that lists all the directories and subdirectories on the current disk and shows how they are organized. By moving the highlight bar in the window, you can select an individual directory or branch of the tree. Then, you can select commands that will be applied to the selection.

While XTreeGold's display includes only one Directory window, it includes five types of File windows. These are described in

Table 2.1. Once you have selected a File window, you can work with any or all files in that window.

Window Name	Description
Small	Displayed below the Directory window. Lists files in the selected directory.
Expanded	Displayed in place of the Directory window and Small file window. Lists files in the selected directory.
Branch	Displayed in place of the Directory window and Small file window. Lists files in the selected directory and all its subdirectories (available in XTreeGold 2.0 only).
Showall	Displayed in place of the Directory window and Small file window. Lists all files in every directory on the disk.
Global	Displayed in place of the Directory window and Small file window. Lists all files on the disk and every other disk that has been logged (read).

Table 2.1: File windows

To move the highlight bar to a directory or file in a window, use one of the following techniques:

Selecting a directory or file

- Point with the mouse pointer to the directory or file name and click the left mouse button.
- Press the Up Arrow or Down Arrow to scroll through the tree display or file list.
- Press Page Up or Page Down repeatedly to advance or return the tree or list to the next or previous window.
- Press the Home or End key to highlight the first or last item on a tree or list.

Window Selection:
Keyboard and Mouse Techniques

To work with files and directories, you must be able to move around in a window and between windows. Think of the Directory window as home base. While it's displayed, you can move to any of the File windows. Once a File window is displayed, you can only move back to the Directory window. From the Directory window, move to a different File window if you wish.

There is one exception to this rule. You can move from the Small file window to the Expanded file window before returning to the Directory window.

The key combinations in Table 2.2 enable you to select any File window when the Directory window is displayed.

Selecting a File window

Key(s)	*Description*
Enter	Small file window
Enter, Enter	Expanded file window
B	Branch file window
S	Showall file window
G	Global file window

Table 2.2: Selecting File windows

Press Esc to return to the Directory window from any File window.

There are several additional ways to select each window, including more than one mouse technique for each. Later in this step, you will learn how to use the mouse or keystrokes to select windows from either set of menus.

File, Directory, and Disk Information Boxes

Main display information boxes

The main display provides important information about the tasks you perform and your overall file management activities. The *Path identification line* at the top left always shows the current disk and directory path, whether you are working in the Directory window or a File window.

The *File specification box* at the top right shows the file name(s), including wild cards, that XTreeGold uses to determine which files to display in the File window. Select the groups of files you want to work with by entering this file specification. Below the File specification box is the *Disk specification box,* which shows the disk or volume you are working on, along with the number of available bytes. The *Statistics box* is next. It tells you what window is active (Directory, File, Branch, Showall, or Global) and contains statistics about the relevant files, directories, and disks. When the Directory window is active, the Statistics box displays information on the current disk. When the Small or Expanded file window is active, current directory statistics are displayed. When the Branch, Showall, or Global File window is active, statistics for that window are shown. You can determine which window is active by the location of the highlight bar. The information in these three boxes is immediately updated as you make changes to the disk and move around the windows.

Menus

Pull-down menus

The pull-down menus in XTreeGold 2.0 are a significant enhancement over version 1.0. Any command applicable to the current (Directory or File) window is displayed on one of seven pull-down menus. These menus are organized under logical headers displayed in the menu bar. Five of the menus are available in both the Directory and File windows. The commands included depend on the window you're working in. These five pull-down menus are described in Table 2.3.

Menu	Description
XTree	Lists commands for starting applications, getting help, and configuring and exiting XTreeGold.
File	Lists commands that act on single files. Contains many more commands when a File window is active.
Volume	Lists commands that are applied to volumes or disks.
Tag	Lists commands that let you select files and cancel the selection of files to be acted upon by commands.
Window	Lists commands that let you select a window and modify the display.

Table 2.3: Common pull-down menus

The two remaining pull-down menus described in Table 2.4 are displayed only when an associated window is active. They provide commands that are specific to the active window.

Menu	Description
Directory	Lists commands that act on directories. (Displayed only when the Directory window is active.)
Tagged	Lists commands that act on all tagged files in the current File window. (Displayed only when a File window is active.)

Table 2.4: Window-specific pull-down menus

All the commands listed on the pull-down menus are also available from the command menus displayed at the bottom of the screen.

Command menus

If you are a new user, the organization of the command menus at the bottom of the screen may not be apparent, so it is probably best to work with the pull-down menus. Experienced users may want to continue using the command menus since they provide quick access to all the commands and have the same organization as in version 1.0.

The command menus are identified in the lower left corner of the screen as DIR COMMANDS or FILE COMMANDS. Both command menus are subdivided into Standard, Ctrl, and Alt menus. By default, the standard menu is displayed for the active window. It includes commands that apply to windows, and some of the commands that apply to single directories, volumes, or files. The Ctrl menu is displayed when you press the Ctrl key. It displays commands that act on multiple directories or files. The Alt menu is displayed when you press the Alt key. It displays the program's most advanced commands.

Command Selection: Keyboard and Mouse Techniques

There's more than one method for selecting a command. Here are the fastest mouse and keyboard techniques for selecting from each menu.

Pull-Down Menu Command Selection

Selecting with a mouse

If you are using a mouse, the fastest way to select a command from the pull-down menus is to point to the top of the screen and click the left mouse button, then click the left mouse button on the menu header, then click again on the command.

As you become more familiar with the menu arrangement, you will be able to click at the header location at the top of the screen and open the menu of choice in one step.

Selecting with keys

To use keystrokes to select a command, press F10 to display the menus, press the Right or Left Arrow to open the menu of choice, and then press the highlighted "hotkey" shown. The pull-down menus also list accelerator keys to the right of commands. You can use accelerator keys to select menu options without having to open the menus.

Command Selection From Command Menus

To use the mouse to select a command from the menus at the bottom of the screen:

Selecting with a mouse

- For a standard menu, click the left mouse button on the command.

- For a Ctrl menu, first click the left mouse button in the area that says DIR COMMANDS or FILE COMMANDS to display that menu and then click the left mouse button on the command.

- For an Alt menu, first double-click the left mouse button in the area that says DIR COMMANDS or FILE COMMANDS to display the Alt menu and then click on the command.

To use keys to select a command from the menus at the bottom of the screen:

Selecting with keys

- For a standard menu, press the highlighted letter key or function key shown.

- For a Ctrl menu, first press and hold the Ctrl key and then press the highlighted letter key or function key shown.

- For an Alt menu, first press and hold the Alt key and then press the highlighted letter key or function key shown.

Responding to Prompts

Some commands are executed as soon as you select them, while others require additional information. For example, if you select the *Copy* command to copy a file, you must also indicate where you want to copy the file to. Whenever additional information is required, an ellipsis (three dots, like this...) appears next to the command in the pull-down menu. There is no indicator of additional prompts on the command menu.

XTreeGold always prompts you for any needed information or action. Prompts appear at the bottom of the screen, where the command menu is usually displayed. The location of the prompts is the same, whether you've selected a command from a pull-down or command menu. You can always type the needed information, and most of the time you confirm your entry by pressing Enter. Standard editing and cursor keys (Home, End, Arrows, Backspace, Delete, and Insert) are available. You may also select from any of the options XTreeGold displays by clicking it and then clicking *ok* displayed in the prompt line.

In some cases you can enter or select the default by simply pressing Enter or clicking the left mouse button on *ok*. For example, press Enter or select *ok* to keep the same file name when copying, or to copy to the same destination as in the last copy operation.

Command Selection Shortcuts

Additional helpers for responding to prompts are the command history and the Destination directory window.

The Command History

When a command requires additional information, your entry is automatically saved for future use. At your request, XTreeGold displays the last sixteen entries for any command in a command history window. You can select any item from the history. This is often quicker than typing a response to a prompt and also guarantees you'll enter the response correctly the first time.

Selecting from the command history

When you see ↑*history* displayed in the prompt line, you can display the command history by pressing the Up Arrow key or clicking the left mouse button on *history*. Then use one of the following techniques to select an entry.

- Click the left mouse button on the entry of choice with the mouse.
- Use the Up or Down Arrow to highlight the entry, and press Enter.

Your choice is displayed in the prompt line. You still have to confirm it by clicking the left mouse button on *ok* or pressing Enter.

The Destination Directory Window

Whenever you are prompted for a destination you will see *F2 point* displayed in the prompt line. Selecting this option displays the Destination directory window, where you can select the disk (with the mouse or a key) and highlight the directory that you want entered in the prompt line. This guarantees that the correct path name and syntax are entered even if you have forgotten them.

Step 3

File Selection Techniques

XTreeGold can apply a command to any single directory or file that is selected with the highlight bar. To apply a command to more than one file at a time, you must first select all the files you want to work with and then apply a command. This step covers the many techniques for selecting files.

Setting the File Specification

The File specification box lists all the files displayed in the File window that may be acted upon. When you start XTreeGold, you will see the default file specification *.* in the File specification box. This means that you can select all files on every disk.

To change the file specification and thereby limit the files you work with at one time, select the *File specification* command. Enter any file name or names, using, if you wish, the wild cards * and ?. Up to 28 different file names may be entered, separated by commas.

Changing the file specification

Suppose, in the following action, that you want to work with some .WP and .DOC files. Select the *File specification* (also called *Filespec*) command from the Window pull-down menu, Standard directory command menu, or Standard file command menu.

If you are using XTreePro Gold 1.0, there are no pull-down menus. Try this action from the command menus.

1. Press F, or open the Window pull-down menu and click the left mouse button on *File specification*.
2. Type ***.WP, *.DOC** and press Enter. The new file specification appears in the File specification box; only files with .WP or .DOC extensions now appear in the File window, as shown in Figure 3.1.
3. Press F or click the left mouse button on *Filespec*.

18 *Up & Running with XTreeGold 2*

```
Path: D:\WP50                                          7-27-91  8:34:14 am
ORDERWPG.DOC      XTGUG7  .DOC      XTGUGZ  .WP      FILE *.WP *.DOC
OUTLINE .DOC      XTGUG8  .DOC      XTGUG3  .WP
PS1     .DOC      XTGUG9  .DOC      XTGUG4  .WP      DISK  D:GRAPHIC
PS2     .DOC      BACKUP  .WP       XTGUG5  .WP      Available
PS3     .DOC      ENVELOP .WP       XTGUG6  .WP          Bytes   23,992,320
PS4     .DOC      GRAFT   .WP       XTGUG7  .WP
PS5     .DOC      INDEX   .WP       XTGUG8  .WP      DIRECTORY Stats
PS6     .DOC      LABEL   .WP       XTGUG9  .WP      Total
TESTWW  .DOC      MAILLST .WP       YACHT   .WP          Files              144
XTGUG0  .DOC      MEMO1107.WP                            Bytes        2,653,828
XTGUG1  .DOC      MEMO1108.WP                        Matching
XTGUG10 .DOC      MEMOMARS.WP                            Files               47
XTGUG11 .DOC      MER     .WP                            Bytes          900,324
XTGUG12 .DOC      README  .WP                        Tagged
XTGUG2  .DOC      XTGUG0  .WP                            Files                0
XTGUG3  .DOC      XTGUG1  .WP                            Bytes                0
XTGUG4  .DOC      XTGUG10 .WP                        Current File
XTGUG5  .DOC      XTGUG11 .WP                            ORDERWPG.DOC
XTGUG6  .DOC      XTGUG12 .WP                            Bytes            6,155

FILE           Attributes  Copy   Delete  Edit   Filespec  Invert   Log disk  Move
COMMANDS       New date    Open   Print   Rename Tag       Untag    View      eXecute  Quit
 ⏎ tree        F7 autoview F8 split        F9 menu  F10 commands     F1 help  ESC cancel
```

Figure 3.1: Expanded file window with files matching the file specification

4. This time don't type anything; just press Enter. The default file specification *.* reappears.

Selecting Files to Be Acted Upon

Tagging files

In XTreeGold you select groups of files for subsequent command operation by tagging them before you select the command. Tagging marks files as selected and keeps them marked until you are finished working with them. Once they are selected, a diamond (♦) is placed to the right. When you finish working with the files, you untag them so that commands you select are no longer applied to these files. You can select files individually, by directory, by disk, or by volume. You can select files in any active window.

When you have tagged the files you want to work with, select any command shown on the Tagged pull-down menu or Ctrl file command menu. The command is applied to all the tagged files at once.

Selecting Files Individually: Keyboard and Mouse Techniques

There are several keyboard and mouse techniques for tagging files. Use whichever you find most efficient.

Tagging Files

Select the *File* command from the Tag pull-down menu, or the *Tag* command from the Standard file command menu, when any File window is active. Try out the following techniques for tagging files.

1. Use the left mouse button or Arrow keys to highlight a file.
2. Open the Tag pull-down menu and either click the left mouse button on *File* or press F.
3. Use the left mouse button or Arrow keys to highlight another file.
4. Press T or click the left mouse button on *Tag* in the command menu.

Tagging techniques

For mouse users only:

1. Click on the file with the right mouse button.
2. Press and hold the right mouse button while you drag the pointer down the file list.

The right mouse button toggles between Tag and Untag.

Untagging Files

With a File window active, select the *File* command listed under the subheader Untag on the Tag pull-down menu, or select the *Untag* command from the Standard file command menu. Try out the following techniques for untagging files.

Untagging techniques

1. Use the left mouse button or Arrow keys to highlight a file that is marked with a diamond.
2. Open the Tag pull-down menu. Click the left mouse button on the second *File* option, or highlight it with the Down Arrow key and press Enter.
3. Use the left mouse button or Arrow keys to highlight another tagged file.
4. Press U, or click the left mouse button on *Untag* in the command menu at the bottom of the screen.

For mouse users only:

1. Click the right mouse button on a tagged file.
2. Press and hold the right mouse button while you drag the pointer down a list of tagged files.

You can also untag all the tagged files at once. Several methods are described later in this step.

Selecting Files Within Directories: Keyboard and Mouse Techniques

When you want to work with all the files in a directory that match the file specification, you can select all of them at once.

The quickest way to select files from one or more directories depends on the window you are working in and whether you want to tag files in one directory or several directories. If a File window is active and you want to work with files that are all in one directory, use the first of the two methods described in the Action below. If you want to work with files that are in more than one directory, or if the directory window is active, use the second method.

Tagging Files in One Directory

Select the *All in window* command from the Tag pull-down menu, or the *Tag* command from the Ctrl file command menu,

File Selection Techniques   21

when any File window is active. Use any of the following tagging techniques.

- Open the Tag pull-down menu, and click *All in window* or press A.
- Click the left mouse button on FILE COMMANDS and then on *Tag* in the command menu.
- Press Ctrl-T.

Tagging techniques

Untagging Files in One Directory

With a File window active, select the *All in window* command that's listed under the subheader Untag in the Tag pull-down menu. Or select the *Untag* command from the Ctrl file command menu. Use any of the following untagging techniques.

Untagging techniques

- Using a mouse, open the Tag pull-down menu. Click the left mouse button on the second occurrence of *All in window*.
- Press F10 to display the pull-down menus. Using the direction keys, open the Tag pull-down menu. Press the Down Arrow key to highlight the second occurrence of *All in window,* then press Enter.
- Click the left mouse button on FILE COMMANDS and then on *Untag* in the command menu.
- Press Ctrl-U.

Tagging Files in More Than One Directory

Use this approach if the Directory window is already active or if you'll be working with the files in more than one directory. Select the *Directory files* command from the Tag pull-down menu or, when the Directory window is active, the *Tag* command from the Standard directory command. Give all the techniques a try.

Tagging techniques

1. Use the left mouse button or Arrow keys to highlight a directory.
2. Open the Tag pull-down menu, and click *Directory files* or press D.
3. Use the left mouse button or Arrow keys to highlight another directory.
4. Press T, or click *Tag* in the command menu.

For mouse users only:

1. Click on the directory with the right mouse button.
2. Press and hold the right mouse button while you drag the mouse pointer down the directory tree.

Using either method, continue until you have tagged all the files in the directory. Notice that the files for the directory, which are displayed in the Small file window, are all marked with diamonds. Notice also that the highlight bar moves down as you tag or untag the entire directory.

Untagging Files in More Than One Directory

With the Directory window active, select the *Directory files* command under the subheader Untag on the Tag pull-down menu. Or select the *Untag* command from the Standard directory command menu. Give all the techniques a try.

Untagging techniques

1. Use the left mouse button or Arrow keys to highlight a directory.
2. Open the Tag pull-down menu. Under the subheader Untag, click the *Directory files* option, or use the Down Arrow to highlight it and then press Enter.
3. Use the left mouse button or Arrow keys to highlight another directory.

File Selection Techniques

4. Press U, or click the left mouse button on *Untag* in the command menu.

For mouse users only:

1. Click the right mouse button on a directory in which all files are tagged.
2. Press and hold the right mouse button while you drag the mouse pointer down the directory tree.

The right mouse button toggles the tag state of files. If you use it on directories whose files are not tagged, the files will become tagged and you may later accidentally apply a command to them.

Selecting All Files on a Disk: Keyboard and Mouse Techniques

When the Directory window is active, it's easy to select or cancel selection of all the files on the current disk or volume.

Tagging All Files

Select the *All disk files* command from the Tag pull-down menu or the *Tag* command from the Ctrl directory command menu.

Untagging All Files

Select the *All disk files* command that's listed under the subheader Untag from the Tag pull-down menu. Or select the *Untag* command from the Ctrl directory command menu.

It's a good idea to use the *All disk files* untagging command whenever you've finished working with a group of files. This guarantees that you won't accidentally leave some files tagged and later apply a command to them unintentionally.

Selecting Files Within Windows: Keyboard and Mouse Techniques

When working in a Branch, Showall, or Global file window, you can select either individual files or all files in the window. Use either of the two Tag file commands that are available when the File window is active.

Tagging files in a window

Select any window. Then:

- To tag a single highlighted file in the window, select the *File* command from the Tag pull-down menu or the *Tag* command from the Standard file command menu.

- To tag all the files in the window, select the *All in window* command from the Tag pull-down menu or the *Tag* command from the Ctrl file command menu. This command tags all files, no matter what directory or disk they are located on.

See Step 2 for window selection techniques.

Step 4

Disk and Directory Selection

When you start XTreeGold, the current disk or volume (or an alternative one that you indicate) is immediately logged, and the directory tree for the volume is displayed in the Directory window. All the directories in the volume are also logged. When you highlight a directory, the contents are displayed in the Small file window. This is the default method of logging.

Logging enters into temporary memory the information about files and directories that XTreeGold needs in order to apply commands to them. In this step you will learn how to log the volumes that you want to work with.

Logging Disks: Using the Menus

XTreeGold provides two commands for logging. One lets you select a disk or volume and, in one operation, log all its directories and files. The other lets you select, from a menu of log options, how you want to log a disk.

A Complete Log

To log all the directories and files on a disk, select the *Log disk* command from the Volume pull-down menu, or the *Log* command from either the Standard directory command menu or Standard file command menu.

Choose any of the following methods.

- Open the Volume pull-down menu and either click the left mouse button on *Log disk* or press L.
- Click on *Log* in the command menu.
- Press L.

Logging a disk

A list of all available volumes and disk drives appears in the prompt line. Select any letter by clicking or typing it. The disk or volume you select is logged and its directory tree appears in the Directory window.

The volume that was previously logged remains logged, although it is not currently displayed.

Additional Logging Options

XTreeGold 2.0 also provides three ways to log only the parts of the volume that you want to work with. This way, XTreeGold does not hold unnecessary information in memory. These three logging options (see Table 4.1) can only be applied to the current volume.

Partial logging

Option	Description
Tree only	Logs or relogs the directory tree structure, beginning at the highlighted directory. Does not log the files in the directories.
One level	Logs or relogs one level of the tree structure, beginning at the highlighted directory. Logs the files in the highlighted directory only.
Branch	Logs the tree structure, beginning at the highlighted directory. Logs all the files in all the directories on the branch.

Table 4.1: Options available with the Log options command

If a disk is fully logged, you can use the *Tree only* and *One level* options to release information from memory. If a disk is partially logged, you can use the *Branch* and *One level* options to log additional directories and files.

The partial logging options are available when you select the *Log options* command from the Volume pull-down menu or the *Log* command from the Alt directory command menu. The Directory window must be active.

Choose any of the following methods for partial logging. Begin by highlighting a directory, then:

- Open the Volume pull-down menu and either click *Log options* or press o.
- Double-click the left mouse button on DIR COMMANDS and then click the left mouse button on *Log* in the command menu.
- Press Alt-L.

A list of available Log options appears in the prompt line. Select any option by clicking on it with the left mouse button or by typing the highlighted letter.

XTreeGold displays two additional logging options on the prompt line. One, the *Disk drive* option, lets you Log a disk and release all other logged disks at the same time. The other, the *Refresh directory* option, is identical to the *Relog directory* command. It lets you refresh the file display for the current directory.

Partial logging

Partial Logging From the Command Line

You can also specify a partial logging option from the DOS prompt when you start XTreeGold 2.0. The command line options are like those for the *Log options* command, but operate either on an unlogged volume that you specify or on the current volume as the default. The options available for partial logging from the command line are described in Table 4.2.

Command line options

Option	Description
/LT (Tree)	Logs the entire tree structure. Does not log the files in the directories.
/L1 (1 level)	Logs one level of the tree structure, beginning at the root directory. Logs the files in the root directory only.

Table 4.2: Command line log options

Practice using a command line option.

1. Quit XTreeGold by selecting *Quit* from the Standard command menu or XTree pull-down menu.
2. If the C:>XTGOLD prompt is not displayed, type **CD XTGOLD** and press Enter.
3. Restart XTreeGold with the *One level* log option by typing **XTGOLD /L1** and pressing Enter. Only the top level directories are logged, as shown in Figure 4.1.
4. Scroll the tree with the Arrow keys or mouse.

The message *Dir Not Logged* is displayed in the Small file window as you highlight each directory (with the exception of the root directory).

Select the *Log options* command and then use the *Branch* and *One level* options to log additional directories and files.

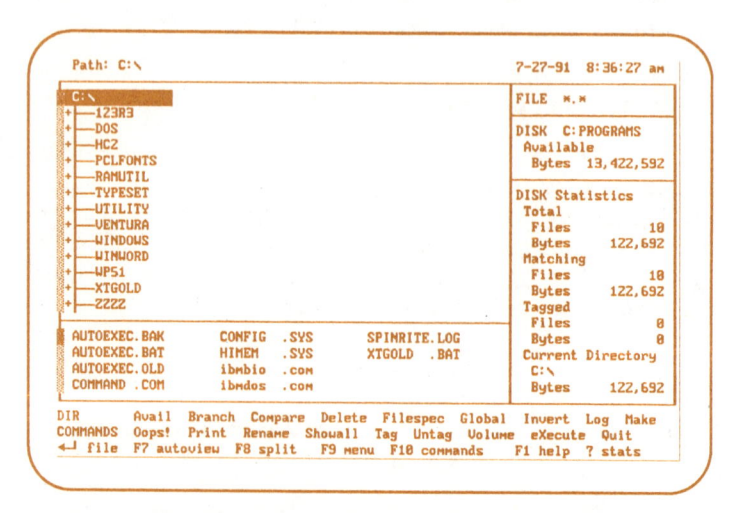

Figure 4.1: Directory tree logged one level down with /L1

Releasing Disks from Memory: Using the Menus

XTreeGold enables you to log and keep information in memory for a maximum of 28 disks and volumes. However, once you are through working on a disk, it may be more efficient to release the information. The less information you maintain in memory, the faster XTreeGold can work. Also, when working with several volumes at once, it simplifies matters to keep only those volumes logged.

As with logging, several full and partial release methods are available to you.

Releasing a Disk or Volume

Select the *Release* command from the Volume pull-down menu or the *Release disk* command from the Alt directory or Alt file command menu.

Use any of the following methods.

- Open the Volume pull-down menu, and click the left mouse button on *Release* or press R.
- Double-click the left mouse button on DIR COMMANDS or FILE COMMANDS to access the command menu, and then click the left mouse button on *Release disk*.
- Press Alt-R.

If a File window is active, XTreeGold displays a list of logged drives in the prompt line. Select any drive letter by clicking or typing it. If the Directory window is active, XTreeGold displays three options. First select *Disk drive* in the prompt line and then select a drive letter.

You can release the current drive by bypassing this prompt and pressing Enter.

Releasing a disk

Partially Releasing a Disk or Volume

To see the two partial release options, *Branch* and *Files in branch*, select the *Release* command from the Volume pull-down menu or, when the Directory window is active, the *Release disk* command from the Alt directory command menu (in version 2.0 only).

Partial releasing

Option	Description
Branch	Releases the branch beginning at the highlighted directory, including all files and directories.
Files in branch	Releases the files in the branch beginning at the highlighted directory, but does not release the directories.

Table 4.3: Options available with the Release or Release disk command

Remember, if you select the *Log options* command, you can log a disk and release all others from memory by using the *Disk drive* option.

Switching Disks

Once you have logged more than one disk or partial disk, you can easily switch to any logged disk. Select either the *Switch to disk* command, the *Next disk* command from the Volume pull-down menu, or the < > select keys from the Standard directory command menu, or just press the < or > key. With XTreePro Gold 1.0, use the Plus or Minus keys instead to scroll through logged disks.

The *Next disk* command and select keys cycle through logged drives without displaying additional prompts. Use the *Switch to disk* command when you have logged several disks and want to quickly select one. The keyboard equivalent of *Switch to disk* is Ctrl-L.

Step 5
Customizing the Tree Display

Step 4 described the different log and release commands and options used to select files and directories. In Step 5 you will learn how to expand and collapse the directory tree with a few keystrokes or mouse clicks, bypassing the menus entirely.

Depending on your tasks, you may want to modify the tree display as your work session proceeds. Or you may need to log and release portions of several volumes, so that only the directories and files you are working with are held in memory. XTreeGold 2.0 provides an assortment of mouse and keystroke techniques to suit your needs. These techniques are only available to XTreeGold 2.0 users.

Tree Symbols

You have probably noticed the symbols to the left of directory names in the tree as you logged and collapsed parts of the tree (see Figure 5.1).

```
C:\
  ├─123R3
+ │  ├─ADDINS
  │  ├─TEMP
+ │  └─WYSIWYG
  ├─DOS
  ├─HC2
  ├─PCLFONTS
  ├─RAMUTIL
  ├─TYPESET
. ├─UTILITY
  ├─VENTURA
+ ├─WINDOWS
  └─WINWORD

Dir Not Logged
```

Figure 5.1: A partially logged directory tree

The symbols shown in Table 5.1 indicate the logging status of a directory in XTreeGold.

Symbol	Description
blank space	The directory has been logged.
. (dot)	The directory has been logged, but its subdirectories are not displayed.
+ (plus sign)	The directory is not logged. It may have been logged and then released.

Table 5.1: Symbols indicating directory status

It's important to understand the difference between what's not displayed and what's not logged. If directories and files are not logged, no command you choose will impact them. On the other hand, if you collapse the display and then use the *Tag* command to tag all the files on a volume, you will tag files in collapsed directories even though they aren't displayed.

Expanding and Collapsing the Directory Tree Display

With the mouse

The quickest way to collapse and then restore the directory tree display is to:

1. Place the mouse pointer to the left of the top level directory in a branch. Make sure the pointer is between the scroll bar and the tree.
2. Double-click the left mouse button. The directory tree collapses, and a dot appears at the pointer position.
3. Place the mouse pointer in the same spot again (it will be on the . this time).
4. Double-click the left mouse button again. The display is restored and a blank space is inserted next to the tree.

Customizing the Tree Display   33

To collapse and restore the directory tree display with keystrokes:

1. Use the Arrow keys to highlight the top level directory in a branch.
2. Press F6. The display collapses, and a dot appears to the left of the directory. If no dot appears next to a directory, there are no subdirectories to collapse.
3. Now highlight the same directory and press F6 again. The display is restored and a blank space is inserted next to the tree.
4. Press the Home key. This highlights the root directory.
5. Now press F5. The tree collapses so that only the first level subdirectories are displayed.

Either pressing F6 or double-clicking the left mouse button collapses the tree display to the current subdirectory level. The F5 key provides an intermediate level of change by collapsing or expanding to one level below the current subdirectory level.

The F5 and F6 keys are not shown on the menu.

Partially Logging and Releasing the Tree

Additional keys and mouse techniques are available for quick logging and releasing.

Try both of the following methods to quickly log an unlogged directory:

- Place the mouse pointer on the directory and click the left mouse button, then click anywhere in the Small file window.
- Use the Arrow keys to highlight the directory and press Enter.

With keystrokes

Quick logging

With both of these methods, the Directory window remains active and the files for the directory are displayed in the Small file window.

First level logging

Try both of the following methods to log the files and first level subdirectories in an unlogged directory:

- Place the mouse pointer on the + next to the directory and click the left mouse button.
- Use the Arrow keys to highlight the directory and press the Plus key (either Plus key will work).

The files for the highlighted directory appear in the Small file window, and one level of subdirectories is displayed.

There's only one quick way to fully log an entire branch.

Branch logging

Try this: Use the Arrow keys to highlight the top level directory, and press the Asterisk key.

Now, no symbols appear to the left of any directory in the branch, because it is fully logged.

To perform a full log on a disk, press Home to highlight the root directory and then press the Asterisk key.

There's also only one quick way to fully release an entire branch.

Branch releasing

Try this: Use the Arrow keys to highlight the top level directory, and press the Minus key (either Minus key will work).

Notice the + symbol to the left of the top level directory in the branch. This indicates that it is not logged, and the words *Dir Not Logged* appear in the Small file window.

Practice using the keyboard and mouse techniques to customize your tree display.

1. Press the Home key to highlight the root directory. Now press the Minus key.
2. Press Enter to log the root directory to one level.
3. Double-click the left mouse button on an unlogged directory. Now press the Asterisk key.
4. Place the mouse pointer to the left of the directory you expanded in #3 and double-click the left mouse button to collapse the directory. Now double-click again in the same spot.
5. Use the Arrow keys to select another directory and press the Plus key to log the directory. Now press the Asterisk key.
6. Use the Arrow keys to select the directory that you expanded in step #5, and press F6. Now press F6 again.

Step 6

Copying and Backing Up

XTreeGold provides three commands for copying files:

- The *Copy* command, for copying one file.
- The *Copy files* (Ctrl-Copy) command, for copying all tagged files in the current File window.
- The *Copy with paths* (Alt-Copy) command, for copying all tagged files in the current File window and for copying or maintaining the directory structure of the files.

All are available to XTreePro Gold 1.0 users from the command menus.

This step shows you how to use each of these commands for copying files and backing up directories, branches, and volumes.

Backing up Files and Directories

The first step in copying a file is to select it by highlighting it. Once a file is selected, you can use the *Copy* command to copy it to any location on any disk or volume. If you want to copy more than one file to a specific location:

1. Tag all the files.
2. Display the files in the most suitable File window.
3. Select the *Copy files* command or *Copy with paths* command to copy all the files to any location.

When you select any Copy command, the ↑ *history* and the *F2 point* options are always displayed in the prompt line. Practice using these options in the examples given in this step. They will usually save you time and keystrokes.

Before continuing with this step, put a blank, formatted disk in your disk drive (we assume it's called A:). By the way, don't be

Copying files

concerned about wasting disk space by unnecessarily copying files as you work through this step. In Steps 7 and 8 you'll learn how to move and delete unneeded files.

Copying Individual Files

With any File window active, select the *Copy* command from either the File pull-down menu or the Standard file command menu.

Try this:

1. Use the left mouse button or Arrow keys to highlight a file.
2. Open the File pull-down menu and click the left mouse button on *Copy* or press C.
3. Press Enter to copy the file while keeping the file name the same.
4. Press F2 to display the Destination directory window.
5. Type L or click the left mouse button on *Log disk* in the prompt line to log the disk that you inserted in your disk drive.
6. Type A or click the left mouse button on *A* in the prompt line.
7. Press Enter or click the left mouse button on *ok* in the prompt line to confirm the destination.
8. Press Enter or click the left mouse button on *ok* in the prompt line to confirm the copy operation.

You can quickly copy another file to the same location from another directory.

1. Use the left mouse button or Arrow keys to highlight a file.
2. Click the left mouse button on *Copy* in the command menu, or press C.

Copying and Backing Up 39

3. Press Enter to copy the file while keeping the file name the same.

4. Press Enter or click the left mouse button on *ok* in the prompt line to confirm the destination shown. XTreeGold uses the last destination as the default until you indicate another or end your session.

5. Press Enter or click the left mouse button on *ok* in the prompt line to confirm the copy operation.

In the course of copying files, you will eventually see the message *Error: Insufficient disk space*. Press Enter or click *ok* to view your options:

- Insert another disk and press Enter to continue.

- Insert another disk, press F2 to format it, and press Enter to continue.

- Select *Skip file* in the prompt line. This lets you copy smaller files that may fit on the disk.

- Press Enter to select another disk drive or volume as the destination.

Additional prompts are displayed as needed.

Copying Selected Files in a Window

Select the *Copy files* command from the Tagged pull-down menu, or the *Copy* command from the Ctrl file command menu. These commands copy all tagged files in any File window to a destination of your choice.

This practice session shows you how to copy selected files from anywhere on the current volume to the disk in the A: drive.

Try this:

1. Start with the Directory window active and select the Showall file window by selecting *Showall* from the command menu.

2. Tag the first 10 files in the list, either by highlighting each and selecting *Tag* from the command menu or by dragging the mouse pointer down the list while holding the right mouse button.

As the highlight bar moves down the file list, the path shown in the path line changes accordingly.

3. Press Ctrl-C, or open the Tagged pull-down menu and click the left mouse button on *Copy all*.

4. Press Enter. This copies the files and keeps the file names the same.

5. Press the Up Arrow key or click the left mouse button on *history*. Select A:\ from the history window by clicking on it with the left mouse button or by highlighting it and pressing Enter.

6. Press Y, or click the left mouse button on *Yes*, to replace existing files.

Backing Up a Directory

To back up a directory, you use the same command but a different File window and tagging method. You might also want to put another disk in the A: drive.

1. Start with the Directory window active and, using the left mouse button or Arrow keys, select the directory you want to back up.

2. Press T, or open the Tag pull-down menu and click the left mouse button on *Directory files*.

Copying and Backing Up　**41**

The highlight bar moves down when you tag all the files in a directory with the Directory window active.

3. Highlight the directory again, and press Enter or click the left mouse button in the Small file window.

4. Press Ctrl-C, or click the left mouse button on FILE COMMANDS and then on *Copy* in the command menu.

5. Press Enter. This copies the files and keeps the file names the same.

6. Press F2 to display the Destination directory window.

7. Type L, or click the left mouse button on *Log disk* in the prompt line, to log the disk in your disk drive.

8. Type A, or click the left mouse button on *A* in the prompt line.

9. Press Enter, or click the left mouse button on *ok* in the prompt line, to confirm the destination.

10. Press Enter, or click the left mouse button on *ok* in the prompt line, to confirm the copy operation.

11. Press N, or click the left mouse button on *No*, if you don't want to replace existing files automatically.

12. When you see the prompt *File exists Replace?*, select *Yes* or *No*.

Copying an Entire Branch

When you want to copy the files in an entire branch to another destination or for backup purposes, you will benefit from using the *Copy with paths* command. This copies the directory structure along with the files.

You can use the *Copy with paths* command from the Tagged pull-down menu, or the *Copy* command from the Alt file command menu, to copy all tagged files in any File window, and their directory structure, to a destination of your choice. If necessary, these commands will recreate the directories beneath the destination directory.

XTreeGold 2.0 gives you a choice of two *Copy with paths* methods, displayed in the prompt line. If you choose the *full paths* option, the branch is recreated beneath the destination directory, as shown in Figure 6.1. If you choose the *partial branch paths* option, the files in the parent directory are copied to the destination directory, and the rest of the directory structure is replicated beneath the destination directory, which becomes the new parent, as shown in Figure 6.2.

In the next exercise, you move to the Branch file window first, then highlight all the files in it. If your system's hard disk has more than one volume, copy from one volume to another this time, instead of to a disk drive. It will be much faster.

If you are using version 1.0, you must first tag files in each directory individually and then select the Showall tagged files window (Ctrl-S). When you have done all this, use the Alt-Copy command to copy all files in a branch.

1. Start with the Directory window active. Use the mouse pointer or Arrow keys to highlight the top level directory in the branch.

```
C:\123R3                        A:\123R3
┌<disk: *.*>─┐                  ┌<disk: *.*>─┐
│C:\         │                  │A:\         │
│ ├─123R3   ←│                  │ └─123R3    │
│ │  ├─ADDINS│                  │    ├─ADDINS│
│ │  ├─TEMP  │                  │    ├─TEMP  │
│ │  └─WYSIWYG│                 │    └─WYSIWYG│
│ ├─DOS     │                   │            │
│ ├─HC2     │                   │            │
│ ├─PCLFONTS│                   │            │
│ ├─RAMUTIL │                   │            │
│ ├─TYPESET │                   │            │
│ ├─UTILITY │                   │            │
│ │  ├─MOUSE│                   │            │
│ │  └─SPINRITE│                │            │
│ └─VENTURA │                   │            │
└───────────┘                   └────────────┘
```

Figure 6.1: A branch copied with the full paths option

Copying and Backing Up 43

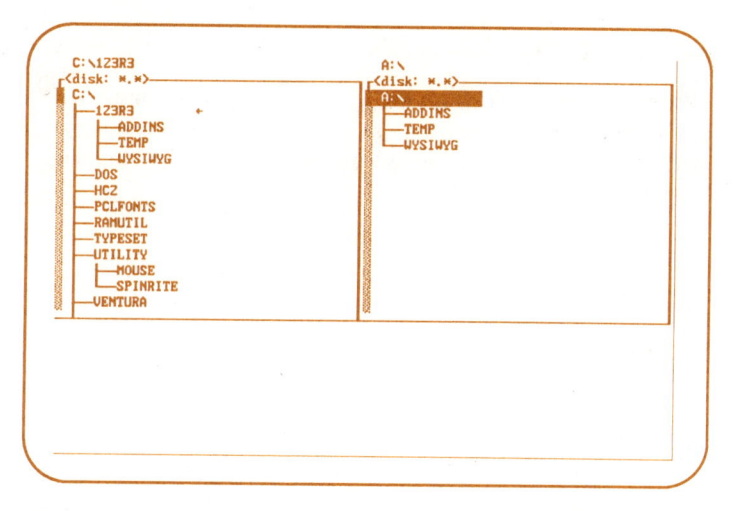

```
C:\123R3
 <disk: *.*>
 C:\
  ├─123R3
  │  ├─ADDINS
  │  ├─TEMP
  │  └─WYSIWYG
  ├─DOS
  ├─HC2
  ├─PCLFONTS
  ├─RAMUTIL
  ├─TYPESET
  ├─UTILITY
  │  ├─MOUSE
  │  └─SPINRITE
  └─VENTURA

A:\
 <disk: *.*>
 A:\
  ├─ADDINS
  ├─TEMP
  └─WYSIWYG
```

Figure 6.2: A branch copied with the partial branch paths option

2. Select *Branch files* from the Window pull-down menu or *Branch* from the Standard directory command menu.

3. Press Ctrl-T, or click the left mouse button on FILE COMMANDS and then on *Tag* in the command menu.

4. Press Alt-C, or open the Tagged pull-down menu and click the left mouse button on *Copy with paths*.

5. Press Enter, or click the left mouse button on *ok* to copy the files while keeping the file name the same.

6. Press the Up Arrow key or click the left mouse button on *history*. Select any destination from the history window by clicking on it with the left mouse button or by highlighting and pressing Enter.

7. Press Y or click the left mouse button on *Yes* to replace existing files.

8. Press Enter or click the left mouse button on *ok* to retain the full paths of the source files and begin the copying process.

Copying an Entire Volume

When you want to copy all the files on a volume for backup purposes, you will benefit from using the *Zip and Arc* command or *Archive files* command instead of one of the Copy commands. Step 15 covers this capability.

Step 7
Deleting Items

This step shows you how to use XTreeGold's Delete commands to delete either files and directories, or the entire contents of a branch or disk.

Deleting Files, Directories, and Branches

XTreeGold provides four commands for deleting files and directories:

- The *Delete* command, for deleting one file.
- The *Delete files* (Ctrl-Delete) command, for deleting all tagged files in the current File window.
- The *Delete* command, for deleting a single directory that contains no files or subdirectories.
- The *Prune* (Alt-P) command, for deleting not only all files and all subdirectories in a branch but also the parent directory of that branch, if you wish.

All four commands are available to XTreePro Gold 1.0 users from the command menus. If you are proceeding through the steps in order, you might want to use this occasion to delete the files you created in Step 6.

Deleting Individual Files

The first step in deleting a file is to select it by highlighting it. Once a file has been selected, you can easily delete it using the *Delete* command. If you want to delete more than one file at a time:

1. Tag all the files.
2. Display the files in the best File window.

Deleting files

3. Select the *Delete files* (Ctrl-Delete) command to delete the files.

With any File window active, select the *Delete* command from the File pull-down menu or the Standard file command menu.

Try this:

1. Use the left mouse button or Arrow keys to highlight a file.
2. Open the File pull-down menu and click the left mouse button on *Delete,* or press D.
3. Press Y or click the left mouse button on *Yes* to delete the file.

If you decide you do not want to delete the selected file(s), select *No* in response to the *Delete this file?* prompt. This immediately cancels the procedure.

Now quickly delete another file in another directory:

1. Use the left mouse button or Arrow keys to highlight a file.
2. Click the left mouse button on *Delete,* or press D in the command menu.
3. Press Y, or click the left mouse button on *Yes* to delete the file.

XTreeGold does not prompt you for additional confirmation when you are deleting only one file, so be certain you want to delete the file before responding *Yes*.

Deleting Selected Files in a Window

Having selected files for deletion by tagging them, use the *Delete files* command from the Tagged pull-down menu or the *Delete* command from the Ctrl file command menu to delete all tagged files.

This practice session will show you how to delete selected files anywhere on the current volume.

Try this:

1. Start with the Directory window active and select the Showall file window by selecting *Showall* from the command menu.

2. Tag the first 10 files in the list by repeatedly selecting *Tag* from the command menu, or by dragging the mouse pointer down the list while holding the right mouse button.

As the highlight bar moves down the file list, the path shown in the path line changes accordingly.

3. Press Ctrl-D or open the Tagged pull-down menu and click the left mouse button on *Delete*.

4. Respond to the prompt *Confirm delete for each file?* by pressing N or clicking the left mouse button on *No*. This deletes all the tagged files in the window.

When you select the *Delete files* command, you are asked if you want to confirm the deletion of each tagged file individually. By selecting *Yes*, you avoid accidental erasure of files. However, the process takes longer, because you must separately confirm the deletion of each file. Selecting *No* results in quick deletion of all tagged files, but does not allow you to double-check your selection.

Deleting All Files in a Directory

You can use the same Delete command to delete all files in a directory. However, you use a different File window and tagging method.

1. Start with the Directory window active and use the left mouse button or Arrow keys to select the directory whose files you want to delete.

2. Press T, or open the Tag pull-down menu and click the left mouse button on *Directory files*.

The highlight bar moves down to the next directory in the tree when you tag all the files in a directory with the Directory window active.

3. Highlight the directory again, and press Enter or click ↵ *files* in the command menu.
4. Press Ctrl-D, or click the left mouse button on FILE COMMANDS and then on *Delete* in the command menu.
5. This time, don't delete the files automatically. Respond to the prompt *Confirm delete for each file?* by pressing Y or clicking the left mouse button on *Yes*.
6. Each time you see the prompt *Delete this file?* select *Yes* or *No*.

You can also quickly delete the contents of a directory by using the Prune command described later in this step.

Deleting a Directory

It's easy to delete a directory that contains no files or subdirectories. With the Directory window active, select the *Delete* command from either the Directory pull-down menu or the Standard directory command menu.

To delete any empty directory, try this:

1. Start with the Directory window active and use the left mouse button or Arrow keys to select the directory you intend to delete.
2. Press D, or open the Directory pull-down menu and click the left mouse button on *Delete*.
3. When the prompt *Delete this directory?* appears, press Y or click the left mouse button on *Yes*.

Deleting Items **49**

XTreeGold will not prompt you for additional confirmation, so think twice before responding *Yes*. If necessary, select *No* to cancel the procedure.

If the directory you try to delete contains files or subdirectories, XTreeGold displays the message *Directory not empty*. Use either the *Delete files* command to delete the files first or the *Prune* command to delete both the files and directory. The only efficient use of the *Delete directory* command is to delete a directory that is already empty.

Deleting Directories, Branches, and Their Contents with Prune

The *Prune* command is the fastest way to delete all the files in a directory or all the files and subdirectories in an entire branch. Once you have deleted the contents of a directory or branch with *Prune*, you can also delete the directory or parent itself.

Use the *Prune* command from the Directory pull-down menu or the Alt directory command menu to delete the contents of an entire directory.

Deleting a Directory With Prune

To delete the contents of a single directory and also delete the directory itself, follow these steps.

1. Start with the Directory window active. Use the left mouse button or Arrow keys to select the directory you want to prune.
2. Press Alt-P, or open the Directory pull-down menu and click the left mouse button on *Prune*.
3. When the prompt *Enter the word PRUNE:* appears, type the word **prune** and press Enter or click the left mouse button on *ok*.

4. The contents of the directory are deleted and the prompt *Delete this directory?* appears. Press Y or click the left mouse button on *Yes* to delete the directory as well.

As you can see, this procedure is much simpler than first tagging and deleting the contents of the directory and then deleting the directory.

Deleting a Branch with Prune

The process for deleting a branch is almost identical to deleting a directory.

1. With the Directory window active, use the left mouse button or Arrow keys to select the top level directory of the branch you want to prune.

2. Press Alt-P, or open the Directory pull-down menu and click the left mouse button on *Prune*.

3. When you see the prompt *Enter the word PRUNE:*, as shown in Figure 7.1, type the word **prune** at the keyboard, and press Enter or click the left mouse button on *ok*.

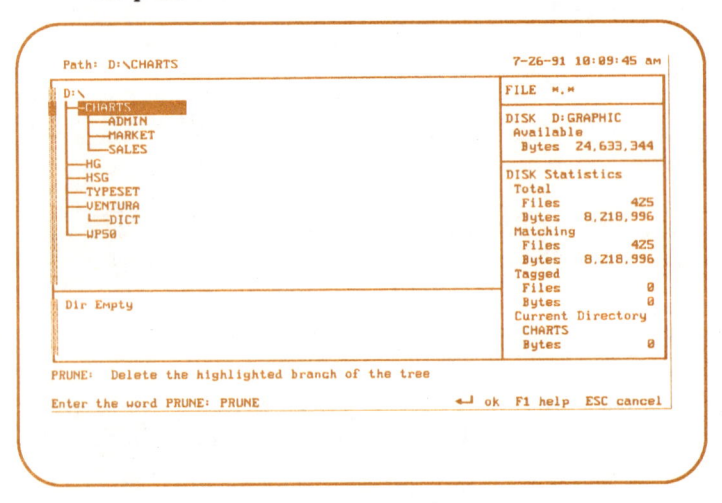

Figure 7.1: Deleting a branch with Prune

4. The contents of the branch are deleted and the prompt *Delete this directory?* appears. Press Y or click the left mouse button on *Yes* to delete the parent directory as well.

Obviously, this procedure is much simpler than first selecting the Branch window, then tagging and deleting the contents of the window, and then deleting each subdirectory in the branch.

Deleting the Contents of a Disk

Use the *Prune* command to delete all the files on a floppy disk whether or not the disk contains subdirectories.

Insert a diskette that contains unneeded files into the A: drive. Try the following:

1. First log the disk. Press L, or open the Volume pull-down menu and click the left mouse button on *Log*. Select *A* from the prompt line. When the disk has been logged, the directory tree appears in the Directory window. The root directory is highlighted.
2. Press Alt-P, or open the Directory pull-down menu and click the left mouse button on *Prune*.
3. At the prompt *Enter the word PRUNE:* type the word **prune.** Press Enter or click the left mouse button on *ok*. The contents of the disk are deleted.

Pruning an unlogged disk

Because the top level directory of the disk is also the root directory of the volume, you are not given the option of deleting this directory.

1. To prune the contents of a disk you have already logged, select the disk by pressing < or > until its tree is displayed in the Directory window. If necessary, use the left mouse button or press Home to highlight the root directory.
2. Press Alt-P, or open the Directory pull-down menu and click the left mouse button on *Prune*.

Pruning a logged disk

3. When you see the prompt *Enter the word PRUNE:* type the word **prune.** Press Enter or click the left mouse button on *ok.* The contents of the disk are deleted.

When pruning an entire disk from the root directory, make sure the current disk is a removable disk, not your hard disk—unless you are planning on deleting everything on your hard disk. If the current disk is a floppy, the Disk specification box shows DISK A: or DISK B:.

Step 8

Moving Items

When XTreeGold moves files to a new location, it first copies the files to that location, then deletes them from the original location. This step shows you how to move files and directories to another location on the same volume or a different volume.

Moving Files, Directories, and Branches

XTreeGold provides four "move" commands:

- The *Move* command, for moving one file at a time to any location.

- The *Move files* (Ctrl-Move) command, for moving all tagged files in the current File window to any location.

- The *Move with paths* (Alt-Move) command, for moving all tagged files in the current File window and for copying or maintaining the directory structure of the files.

- The *Graft* command, for moving a directory or branch, with its contents, to another location on the same volume.

Except for the *Move with paths* command, all these commands are available to XTreePro Gold 1.0 users from the command menus. However, the 1.0 version can only move files to another directory on the same volume.

The first step in moving a file is to select the file by highlighting it. Once the file is selected, the *Move* command can move it anywhere on any disk or volume. If you want to move more than one file to one specific location:

1. Tag all the files.
2. Display the files in the Showall tagged files window.
3. Select the *Move files* or *Move with paths* command to move them all to a location of your choice.

Moving files

Moving directories

As with a file, the first step in moving a directory is to select the directory by highlighting it. Once the directory is selected, the *Graft* command can move it anywhere on the same disk or volume. If you want to move one or more directories and their contents to another volume:

1. Tag all the files in the directories.
2. Display the files in the Showall tagged files window.
3. Select the *Move with paths* command to move them all to a location of your choice.

When any of the move commands are selected, the ↑ *history* and the *F2 point* options are displayed in the prompt line. Practice using these options in the examples in this step. They will usually save you time and keystrokes.

Moving Individual Files

When any File window is active, select the *Move* command from the File pull-down menu or from the Standard file command menu.

Put a blank disk in your disk drive (we assume it's called A:). Then try this:

1. Use the left mouse button or Arrow keys to highlight a file.
2. Open the File pull-down menu, and click the left mouse button on *Move* or press M.
3. Press Enter to move the file while keeping the file name the same.
4. Press F2 to display the Destination directory window.
5. Type L, or click the left mouse button on *Log disk* in the prompt line, to log the disk that you have inserted in your disk drive.
6. Type A, or click the left mouse button on *A* in the prompt line.

Moving Items

7. Press Enter, or click the left mouse button on *ok* in the prompt line, to confirm the destination.

8. Press Enter, or click the left mouse button on *ok* in the prompt line, to confirm the move operation.

Now move another file from another directory to the same location.

1. Use the left mouse button or Arrow keys to highlight a file.

2. Click the left mouse button on *Move* in the command menu, or press M.

3. Press Enter to move the file while keeping the file name the same.

4. Press Enter, or click the left mouse button on *ok* in the prompt line, to confirm the destination shown. XTreeGold uses the destination from the last move operation as the default until you indicate another or end your session.

5. Press Enter, or click the left mouse button on *ok* in the prompt line, to confirm the move operation.

In the course of moving files, you may see the message *Error: Insufficient disk space*. Press Enter or click the left mouse button on *ok* to see your options. You may:

- Insert another disk and press Enter to continue.

- Insert another disk, press F2 to format it, and press Enter to continue.

- Select *Skip file* in the prompt line. This allows you to continue by moving smaller files that may fit on the disk.

- Press Enter to select another disk drive or volume as the destination.

Additional prompts are displayed as needed.

Moving Selected Files in a Window

Use the *Move files* command from the Tagged pull-down menu or the *Move* command from the Ctrl file command menu to move all tagged files in any File window to a destination of your choice.

Moving All Tagged Files in a File Window

This practice session will show you how to move selected files from anywhere on the current volume to the disk in the A: drive.

Try this:

1. With the Directory window active, select the Showall file window by selecting *Showall* from the command menu.

2. Tag the first 10 files in the list either by highlighting each and selecting *Tag* from the command menu or by dragging the mouse pointer down the list while holding the right mouse button.

As the highlight bar moves down the file list, the path shown in the path line changes accordingly.

3. Press Ctrl-M, or open the Tagged pull-down menu and click the left mouse button on *Move files*.

4. Press Enter to move the files while keeping the file names the same.

5. Press the Up Arrow key or click the left mouse button on *history*. Select A:\ from the history window by clicking on A:\ with the left mouse button or by highlighting A:\ and pressing Enter.

6. Press Y or click the left mouse button on *Yes* to replace existing files.

Tagging and Moving All Files in a Directory

To move all the files in a directory, you use the same move command, but a different File window and tagging method. You might also want to put another disk in the A: drive.

Moving Items

1. With the Directory window active, use the left mouse button or Arrow keys to select the directory whose files you want to move.
2. Press T, or open the Tag pull-down menu and click the left mouse button on *Directory files*.

When the Directory window is active, the highlight bar moves down when you tag all the files in a directory.

3. Highlight the directory again, and press Enter or click the left mouse in the Small file window.
4. Press Ctrl-M, or click the left mouse button on FILE COMMANDS and then on *Move* in the command menu.
5. Press Enter to move the files while keeping the file name the same.
6. Press F2 to display the Destination directory window.
7. Type L, or click the left mouse button on *Log disk* in the prompt line. This logs the disk in the A: drive.
8. Type A, or click the left mouse button on *A* in the prompt line.
9. Press Enter, or click the left mouse button on *ok* in the prompt line, to confirm the destination.
10. Press Enter, or click the left mouse button on *ok* in the prompt line, to confirm the move operation.
11. Press *N*, or click the left mouse button on *No*, so that you won't replace existing files automatically.
12. When the prompt *File exists Replace?* appears, select *Yes* or *No*.

If you are using version 2.0, you may want to use the *Move with paths* command (described next) to move files and copy or retain the directory structure. However, if you don't need to preserve the path information, use the *Move files* (Ctrl-M) command. It's faster.

Moving Files to Another Volume

When you want to move the files in an entire branch to another destination, it's best to use the *Move with paths* command to move the directory structure along with the files. This command is only available with XTreeGold 2.0.

Use the *Move with paths* command from the Tagged pull-down menu or the *Move* command from the Alt file command menu to move all tagged files in any File window to any destination. The directory structure moves with the files. If necessary, new directories are created at the destination.

This time highlight all the files in the Branch file window. If your system's hard disk has more than one volume, move files from one volume to another, instead of to a diskette. This will speed up the operation.

1. Start with the Directory window active. Use the left mouse button or Arrow keys to highlight the top level directory in the branch.

2. Select the *Branch files* command from the Window pull-down menu or the *Branch* command from the Standard directory command menu.

3. Press Ctrl-T, or click the left mouse button on FILE COMMANDS and then *Tag* in the command menu.

4. Press Alt-M, or open the Tagged pull-down menu and click the left mouse button on *Move with paths*.

5. Press Enter or click the left mouse button on *ok* to move the files and keep the same file names.

6. Press the Up Arrow key or click the left mouse button on *history*. Select any destination from the history window using the left mouse button or by highlighting and pressing Enter.

7. Press Y, or click the left mouse button on *Yes* to replace existing files.

8. Press Enter, or click the left mouse button on *ok* to begin the move procedure.

Quickly Moving Directories, Branches, and Their Contents with Graft

The easiest way to move all the files in a directory or all the files and subdirectories in an entire branch is with the Graft command. However, the Graft command only lets you move branches to another location on the same disk or volume.

Remember that any directory can be thought of as a branch of the tree and is treated as such by the Graft command.

Use the *Graft* command from the Directory pull-down menu or the Alt directory command menu to move an entire branch, including all its files and subdirectories.

Follow these steps to:

* Move a single directory with its contents to another parent directory on the same volume.
* Move an entire branch with its contents to another parent directory on the same volume.

Start with the Directory window active, then:

1. Select the directory from which to start the graft, using the left mouse button or Arrow keys.
2. Press Alt-G, or open the Directory pull-down menu and click the left mouse button on *Graft*.
3. The prompt *GRAFT subdirectory: to new parent:* appears in the prompt line, and the Destination directory window is displayed (see Figure 8.1). Select the new parent directory with the left mouse button or Arrow keys. As you scroll with the Arrow keys, the destination changes in the prompt line.

Moving a branch or directory

4. Press Enter or click the left mouse button on *ok* to confirm your choice.
5. XTreeGold asks for confirmation again, displaying the prompt *Continue and graft the tree?* Press Y or click the left mouse button on *Yes* to confirm the graft procedure.
6. The branch and its contents are moved to the selected location.

Figure 8.1: Moving a branch with Graft

Step 9

Renaming Items

15

This step shows you how to use XTreeGold's commands to rename files, directories, and volumes.

Renaming Files, Directories, and Volumes

XTreeGold provides four commands for renaming files, directories, and volumes:

- The Rename file command, for renaming one file at a time.
- The Rename files (Ctrl-Rename) command, for renaming all tagged files in the current File window.
- The Rename Directory command, for renaming one directory at a time.
- The Volume Name command, for renaming a volume.

All are available to XTreePro Gold 1.0 users from the command menus.

The first step in renaming a file is to select it by highlighting it. Once a file is selected, you can use the *Rename* command to quickly rename it. If you want to rename more than one file:

1. Tag all the files.
2. Display them all in the appropriate File window.
3. Select the *Rename files* command to rename them all.

Renaming files

Renaming Individual Files

With any File window active, select the *Rename* command from the File pull-down menu or from the Standard file command menu.

1. Use the left mouse button or Arrow keys to highlight a file.
2. Open the File pull-down menu, and click the left mouse button on *Rename* or press R.
3. Type in the new filename at the prompt, and press Enter or click the left mouse button on *ok*.

Now quickly rename another file in another directory.

1. Use the left mouse button or Arrow keys to highlight a file.
2. Click *Rename* in the command menu, or press R.
3. Type in the new filename at the prompt, and press Enter or click the left mouse button on *ok*.

Renaming Selected Files in a Window

The *Rename* command from the Tagged pull-down menu, or from the Ctrl file command menu, renames all tagged files in any File window. A wild card in the new file name stands for the part of the old file name that does not change.

Renaming all tagged files in a directory

This practice session shows you how to rename selected files in a directory. A wild card is used to give all the files a *.BAK extension.

Try this:

1. Highlight the directory that contains the files you want to rename. To select the directory, highlight it and press Enter or double-click on the directory with the left mouse button.
2. Tag the files that you want to rename by selecting each and pressing T or by pointing at each and clicking the right mouse button.
3. Press Ctrl-R, or open the Tagged pull-down menu and click the left mouse button on *Rename files*.

4. Type in the new filename at the prompt. Use a wild card entry, such as *.BAK, and press Enter or click the left mouse button on *ok*. The renamed files appear in the File window.

Renaming a Directory

To change the name of the current directory, select the *Rename* command from the Directory pull-down menu, or from the Standard directory command menu, when the Directory window is active.

Try this:

1. To select the directory you want to rename, highlight it or point to it and click the left mouse button.

2. Press R, or open the Directory pull-down menu and click the left mouse button on *Rename*.

3. Type in the new directory name at the prompt, and press Enter or click the left mouse button on *ok*. The directory is renamed and displayed in the Directory window.

Renaming a Volume

To change the name of the current volume or disk, select the *Name* command from the Volume pull-down menu, or the *Volume* command from the Standard directory command menu, when the Directory window is active.

Try this:

1. To rename a volume other than the current one, select the desired volume either by logging it (press L and then the drive letter) or by pressing the select keys (< or >) until it is listed in the Disk specification box as the current volume.

2. Press V, or open the Volume pull-down menu and click the left mouse button on *Name*.

3. At the prompt, type in the new volume name and press Enter or click the left mouse button on *ok*. The disk or volume is renamed and displayed in the Disk specification box.

Step 10

Browsing Directories

XTreeGold offers several methods for viewing and searching through the contents of files. This step shows you how to use the Autoview window to quickly browse among and search through any or all files in a directory. All the capabilities covered here are available to XTreePro Gold 1.0 users from the command menus.

Browsing through Directories and Their Files

Browsing is the activity of quickly viewing the contents of one or more files. The Autoview window is the place where you'll browse through files in a selected directory and select files for a closer look. You may also search through all or selected files for a text string you're trying to locate. When you browse through most spreadsheet or database files in the Autoview window, they are automatically formatted by XTreeGold. Document files are displayed in wordwrap format.

Displaying the Autoview Window

Select the *Autoview* command from the Window pull-down menu or the Standard directory or standard file command menu.

Try this: Select the directory that contains the files you want to browse through, either by highlighting it and pressing Enter or by clicking on it with the left mouse button. Then choose any of the following methods.

- Open the Window pull-down menu and click the left mouse button on *Autoview*.
- Open the Window pull-down menu and press A.
- Click the left mouse button on *autoview* in the command menu.
- Press F7.

Opening the Autoview window

When you open the Autoview window, the first 19 lines of the highlighted file appear on the screen, as shown in Figure 10.1. If you open the Autoview window with the Directory window active, the highlighted file is always the first file in the list. If you open the Autoview window with the File window active, the highlighted file is always the current file.

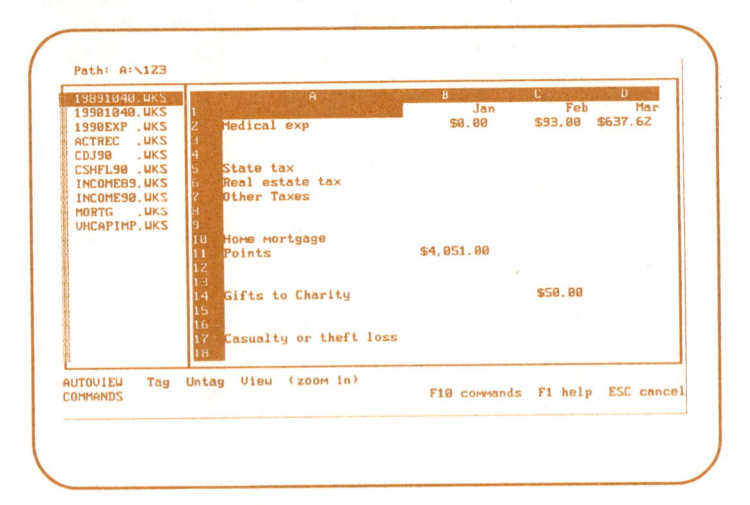

```
Path: A:\123
┌─────────────────┬──────────────────────────────────────────────┐
│ 19891040.WKS    │           A              B        C       D  │
│ 19901040.WKS    │                        Jan      Feb     Mar  │
│ 1990EXP .WKS    │ 2 Medical exp         $0.00   $93.00 $637.62 │
│ ACTREC  .WKS    │ 3                                            │
│ CDJ90   .WKS    │ 4                                            │
│ CSHFL90 .WKS    │ 5 State tax                                  │
│ INCOME89.WKS    │ 6 Real estate tax                            │
│ INCOME90.WKS    │ 7 Other Taxes                                │
│ MORTG   .WKS    │ 8                                            │
│ VHCAPIMP.WKS    │ 9                                            │
│                 │10 Home mortgage                              │
│                 │11 Points           $4,051.00                 │
│                 │12                                            │
│                 │13                                            │
│                 │14 Gifts to Charity              $50.00       │
│                 │15                                            │
│                 │16                                            │
│                 │17 Casualty or theft loss                     │
│                 │18                                            │
├─────────────────┴──────────────────────────────────────────────┤
│ AUTOVIEW   Tag  Untag  View  (zoom in)                         │
│ COMMANDS                              F10 commands F1 help ESC cancel │
└────────────────────────────────────────────────────────────────┘
```

Figure 10.1: The Autoview window

Moving around the Window

Selecting a file to view

After you open the Autoview window, it is easy to change the Autoview selection from the first file in the file list to another listed file. Use either of the following methods:

- Use the Up and Down Arrows to scroll the file list. As you do so, each highlighted file is displayed in turn. There is no need to press Enter.

- Point to any file and click the left mouse button.

To scroll the contents of a file:

- Press Shift and the Up or Down Arrow.
- Position the mouse pointer anywhere within the file display area and hold down the left mouse button. By placing the mouse pointer in the top half of the display area, you can scroll through the contents towards the end of the file. By placing the mouse pointer in the bottom half of the display area, you can scroll through the contents towards the beginning of the file.

Scrolling the file contents

Using the Autoview Menus

The commands described in Table 10.1, which are displayed in the command and pull-down menus, are the only commands that can be applied while the Autoview window is active.

Autoview commands

Menu	Description
XTree	Lists commands for getting help and for exiting the Autoview window. These commands are also available from the Standard Autoview menu.
Tagged	Lists the *Search* and *View* commands, which will act on all tagged files in the Autoview window. These commands are also available from the Ctrl Autoview menu.
Tag	Lists the *Tag* and *Untag* commands on the Standard, Ctrl, and Alt menus.
View	Lists commands that let you change the way an individual file is displayed. You can also select all except *Zoom in* by pressing Shift and the displayed hotkey. Select *Zoom in* from the Standard menu by pressing V (for View).

Table 10.1: Autoview pull-down menus

Zooming in on a File

When working in the Autoview window, you can select a file in the list and display it in the View window without exiting to the main display. (The View window is covered in Step 11.) In the View window, additional searching, place marking, and editing capabilities are available.

If you aren't sure how to locate a document file (perhaps you are working on someone else's system), you can use the Autoview window to browse through the most likely directories. Once you locate the file, you can call up the additional View commands. XTreeGold can then automatically determine the program used to create it. If you wish, select additional commands to format it.

Here's how you can do this:

1. To select the directory, highlight it and press Enter, or double-click on it with the left mouse button.

2. Press F7, or click the left mouse button on *autoview* in the command menu, to open the Autoview window.

3. Press the Down Arrow to browse through each file until you find the one you need. If necessary, press Shift and the Down Arrow together to display more of each file.

4. Press V, or click the left mouse button on *View (zoom in)* in the command menu, to display the file in the View window.

5. Press F, or click the left mouse button on *Formatted* in the command menu, to display the file in its original format.

6. When you are done, press Esc or click the left mouse button on *ESC cancel,* to return to the Autoview window.

If XTreeGold does not recognize the file's format, it displays an error message. Simply select *ok* and choose another formatting option, such as ASCII or Wordwrap.

Searching through Tagged Files

The Search command in the Autoview window lets you search through tagged files for a text string. This helps to locate a specific file or files quickly. Use any of the tag commands to tag files in the list, and then apply the *Search* command to them.

To find all memos and letters written to people at a particular company, try this:

1. Begin with the Autoview window open. Tag all the files by pressing Ctrl-T, or by clicking the left mouse button on AUTOVIEW COMMANDS and then on *Tag* in the command menu.

2. To search all the tagged files, select Search by pressing Ctrl-S or by clicking the left mouse button on AUTOVIEW COMMANDS and then on *Search* in the command menu.

3. At the prompt, type in the company name. It can be up to 31 characters long. Press Enter or click the left mouse button on *ok* to begin the search process.

4. When XTreeGold has finished searching, only the files that contain the company name you entered will remain tagged. To view its contents, use the Arrow keys or left mouse button to highlight the first tagged file.

Step 11

Viewing Files

In the View window, XTreeGold lets you select one or more files for:

- Viewing, which enables you to look at the contents of files in their native formats

- Searching, which you can use to find specific text strings in one or more files

- Gathering and appending, which allows you to copy part of one or more files and paste into another file

- Hex editing, which enables you to edit a file displayed in hexidecimal mode

This step shows you how to use the View window to look through files, display them in their conventional format, and carry out some common information management tasks. XTreePro Gold 1.0 users have access to the same capabilities from the command menus.

XTreeGold automatically formats most spreadsheet and database files in the View window, just as it does in the Autoview window. Word processing files are formatted easily. XTreeGold includes viewers for the most popular word processing, spreadsheet, and database programs.

When you installed XTreeGold 2.0, you chose the viewers to be installed. If you try to display a file for which you have not installed the needed viewer, you will receive an error message. Follow the procedure described in Step 1 if you have to install an additional viewer.

Displaying the View Window

To display the contents of the current file, select the *View* command from either the File pull-down menu or the Standard file command menu. To view all the tagged files, one after another, select the *View* command from the Tagged pull-down menu or from the Ctrl file command menu.

To view one file, select the file by highlighting it. Then, try any of the following methods for opening the view window.

Opening the View window

- Open the File pull-down menu and click the left mouse button on *View* or press V.
- Click the left mouse button on *View* in the command menu, or press V.

Mouse shortcut

- Double-click the right mouse button.

These actions open the View window (see Figure 11.1) and the first 19 lines of the current file appear on the screen. A database or spreadsheet file will already be correctly formatted.

Viewing several files

To view more than one file quickly:

1. Tag all the files you want to display, using any tagging technique.

```
File: D:\WP50\MAILST2.WP                                  ASCII (no mask)

Ms. Deane Swick
12221 San Vincente Blvd
Los Angeles, CA 90021

Ms. Dana Dickinson
2842 Applewood Lane
Castic, CA 91310

Mrs. Margaret Eastman
9705 Delganey
Playa del Rey, CA 90293

Mr. Jeff Field
6030 Orange St.
Los Angeles, CA 90048

VIEW       ASCII  Dump  Formatted  Gather  Hex  Mask  Wordwrap
COMMANDS   F2 F3 F4 F5 F6 goto bookmark  F9 search  SPACE search again
↑↓ scroll  ALT SHFT menus                   F10 commands  F1 help  ESC cancel
```

Figure 11.1: The View window

2. Select the *View* command from the Tagged pull-down menu or from the Ctrl file command menu.

The View window now provides the commands for working with multiple tagged files, and VIEW ALL is displayed in the command menu.

Moving around the Window

Use any of the following methods to scroll the contents of a file:

Scrolling the file contents

- Press the Up or Down Arrow.
- To automatically scroll, press Shift, then press any of the F2 through F6 keys to determine scrolling speed. F2 provides the fastest scrolling, F6 the slowest.
- Place the mouse pointer anywhere on the line at the top or bottom of the file display area and hold down the left button. Placing the mouse pointer at the top scrolls the contents towards the end of the file. Placing the mouse pointer at the bottom scrolls the contents towards the beginning of the file.

The first file in the list is automatically selected for display when you open the View window using either the *View* command from the Tagged pull-down menu or from the Ctrl file command menu. Choosing another file is a simple matter. Either:

Selecting a file to view

- Open the Edit pull-down menu, and click *Next tagged file* or press N.
- In the command menu, click *Next tagged file* or press N.

Using the View Menus

Only the commands displayed in the View command and pull-down menus (see Table 11.1) can be applied while the View window is active. The commands available vary, based on:

- Whether you open the View window using the *View file* command or the *View tagged files* command.
- Whether you are viewing a file in word processing, database, spreadsheet, or other format.

View commands

Menu	Description
XTree	Lists commands for getting help and exiting the View window. These commands are also available from the Standard View menu.
Bookmark	Lists commands for setting and going to bookmarks. The *goto bookmark* commands are available from the Standard View command menu. The *set bookmark* commands are available by pressing Alt to display the Alt View command menu (which is not mouse-selectable).
Edit	Lists the *Search* and *Gather* commands which will act on the file shown in the View window. These commands are also available from the Standard View menu. When applicable, the *Next tagged file* command is also displayed.
View	Lists commands that let you change the way an individual file is displayed. All these commands can also be selected from the Standard menu.

Table 11.1: View pull-down menus

Formatting Files to Meet Specific Needs

XTreeGold's viewing and formatting capabilities enable you to look at files created with various applications without running the applications. This can really save time, and lets you look at files even if your computer doesn't have the application installed.

Viewing Files

If you have installed the available spreadsheet and database viewers, XTreeGold automatically formats all supported spreadsheet and database files when you select the *View* command. XTreeGold does not automatically format word processing files even though the viewers are installed. To format word processing files:

1. With any File window active, select the file by highlighting it with the Up or Down Arrow or by clicking with the left mouse button.

2. Press V, or click *View* in the command menu, to open the View window.

3. Press F, or click *Formatted* in the command menu. XTreeGold analyzes the file and then formats it, if it recognizes the file format. A message is displayed while formatting is in progress.

If XTreeGold does not recognize the file and you know it is in a popular word processing format, go back to Step 1 and install the additional viewer that you need.

Formatting word processing files

Special Database and Spreadsheet Capabilities

In addition to viewing and formatting database and spreadsheet files, XTreeGold gives you some additional information about their contents.

- When you highlight any cell in a spreadsheet file, information about the formula for that cell appears at the top of the View window.

- When you highlight any field in a database file, information about the structure of the field appears at the top of the View window.

Viewing the structure of a database file

- When a database file is in the View window, the *Structure* command is included on the View pull-down menu and in the View command menu. This *Structure* command gives you additional information about the database file, as shown in Figure 11.2.

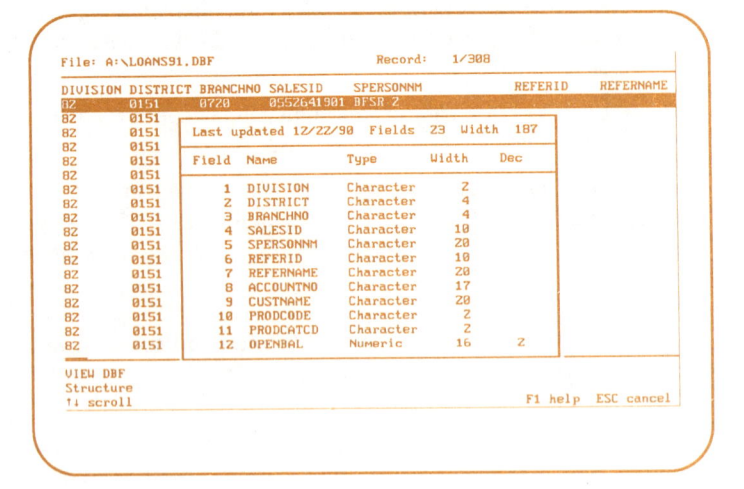

```
File: A:\LOANS91.DBF              Record:   1/308
DIVISION DISTRICT BRANCHNO SALESID     SPERSONNM              REFERID     REFERNAME
82       0151     0720     0552641901 BFSR 2
82       0151
82       0151     Last updated 12/22/90  Fields  23  Width  187
82       0151
82       0151     Field  Name         Type       Width   Dec
82       0151
82       0151       1    DIVISION     Character     2
82       0151       2    DISTRICT     Character     4
82       0151       3    BRANCHNO     Character     4
82       0151       4    SALESID      Character    10
82       0151       5    SPERSONNM    Character    20
82       0151       6    REFERID      Character    10
82       0151       7    REFERNAME    Character    20
82       0151       8    ACCOUNTNO    Character    17
82       0151       9    CUSTNAME     Character    20
82       0151      10    PRODCODE     Character     2
82       0151      11    PRODCATCD    Character     2
82       0151      12    OPENBAL      Numeric      16     2

VIEW DBF
Structure
↑↓ scroll                                            F1 help   ESC cancel
```

Figure 11.2: View DBF Structure display

Gathering and Appending

The *Gather* command is available in the View window. It is a great way to copy from one file to another. Gather lets you select text, cells, or records and then paste or append them to another file. Select the *Gather* command from the Edit pull-down menu or the View command menu to begin this copy and paste procedure.

To copy text from one file to another, try this. The directions begin with the selected file already displayed in the View window.

1. Press G, or click the left mouse button on *Gather* in the Edit command menu.

Viewing Files

2. Press the Arrow keys to highlight the location where you want to begin to copy text. Press Enter to highlight the first line.
3. Press the Down Arrow until you've highlighted the last line you want to copy. Press Enter again.
4. A prompt appears. In response to the prompt, type the name of a new file or an existing file. Press Enter. The selected text is added to the end of that file.

Step 12

Searching through Files

This step shows you how to use the *Search* command to locate a text string in any file on any logged disk. The Search command is available in both XTreeGold 1.0 and 2.0.

Searching for Text Strings

You can search through all tagged files in the active File window for any text string of up to 31 characters. You may use wild card characters, such as * and ?, as long as they are not entered as the first character. XTreeGold does not differentiate between upper and lower case letters as it searches.

When all the tagged files have been searched, only files that contain the text string remain tagged. Within each file, every occurrence of the text string is highlighted. Use the Autoview and View windows to quickly find the highlighted text.

Searching through Files in a Window

You can select the *Search* command, when any File window is active, from either the Tagged pull-down menu or the Ctrl file command menu. Whether you are searching through tagged files in a directory, on a disk, or on all logged disks, the procedure is the same. You simply tag the files you want to search and then select the *Search* command. Remember these pointers for tagging files:

- To search through some or all files in a directory, select the Expanded file window and tag the files.

- To search through some or all files on a branch, select the Branch file window and tag the files.

- To search through some or all files on a disk, select the Showall file window and tag the files.

- To search through some or all files on several disks or volumes, log all the disks. Then, select the Global file window and tag the files.

Searching a directory

You can use the *Search* command to quickly locate all occurrences of a text string in a directory. In the following example, we'll look in a selected directory for an item called GIZMO91.

1. Begin with the Directory window active. Select the directory you want to search through by pointing to it and clicking with the left mouse button or by highlighting it using the Up or Down Arrow.

2. Tag all the files in the directory by pressing T or by opening the Tag pull-down menu and clicking the left mouse button on *Directory files*.

3. Select the File window by pressing Enter or by clicking *files* in the command menu. You can now search through all the files in the window.

4. Select the Search command by pressing Ctrl-S or opening the Tagged pull-down menu and clicking *Search*.

5. At the prompt, type in the text string **gizmo91** and press Enter or click *ok* to begin the search process.

6. When XTreeGold has finished searching, only the files that contain the search string remain tagged. To view all the tagged files in the window, press Ctrl-V or open the Tagged pull-down menu and click the left mouse button on *View*.

Searching the current volume

By using a wild card in the text string, you can locate all references on the current volume to several items that have similar names. Of course, you could search for any single text string with or without a wild card character, and still follow this procedure. To find all references to several project names—PROJECTX, PROJECTY, and PROJECTZ on the current disk—try this.

1. Begin with the Directory window active. Tag all the files on the disk, either by pressing Ctrl-T or by opening the Tag pull-down menu and clicking the left mouse button on *All disk files*.

2. Select the Showall window either by pressing S or by opening the Window pull-down menu and clicking the left mouse button on *Disk files (Showall)*. You can now search through all the files in the Showall window.

3. Select the Search command either by pressing Ctrl-S or by opening the Tagged pull-down menu and clicking the left mouse button on *Search*.

4. At the prompt, type in the project names, using wild card characters instead of the *X, Y,* or *Z*. Type **PROJECT*** and press Enter or click the left mouse button on *ok* to begin the search process.

5. When XTreeGold has finished searching, only files that contain the search string remain tagged. To view all the tagged files in the window, press Ctrl-V or open the Tagged pull-down menu and click the left mouse button on *View*.

Remember that the search techniques we have looked at work in any File window. Just tag all the files you want to look through and choose the best File window. Step 3 contains detailed information on tagging.

You can conduct the same search when the View window is active by selecting the *Search* command from the Edit menu.

Step 13

The Application Menu

This step shows you how to use and modify the Application menu that XTreeGold 2.0 creates during the installation process. For XTreePro Gold 1.0, which does not automatically generate an Application menu during installation, this step shows you how to create, use, and modify a menu.

Creating an Application Menu

Although XTreeGold 2.0 creates an Application menu for you, it may not find all the applications you want to include on the menu, and it may not organize the menu exactly as you like. Yet it is still efficient to let XTreeGold create the menu and then make whatever changes you like.

If you elected not to create a menu automatically when you installed XTreeGold 2.0 but you now want to, go back and follow the instructions in Step 1. It's faster to modify an application menu than to create a new one.

Once the application menu is installed, select the *Application menu* command from the XTree pull-down menu, or press F9 to select the *menu* command from the Standard directory or Standard file command menu.

Displaying the menu

In XTreeGold 2.0, all commands associated with the Application menu (see Figure 13.1) are displayed on pull-down menus, and the headers are already displayed. These commands are described in Table 13.1. There are no command menus at the bottom of the screen at this time. Once you enter editing mode, you will have a command menu to select from.

Up & Running with XTreeGold 2

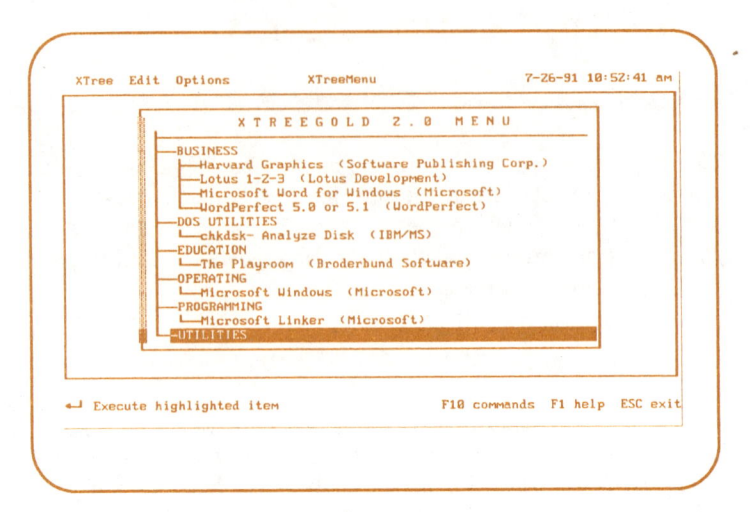

```
XTree  Edit  Options          XTreeMenu              7-26-91 10:52:41 am

                    X T R E E G O L D   2 . 0   M E N U
          ─BUSINESS
          │    ├──Harvard Graphics  (Software Publishing Corp.)
          │    ├──Lotus 1-2-3  (Lotus Development)
          │    ├──Microsoft Word for Windows  (Microsoft)
          │    └──WordPerfect 5.0 or 5.1  (WordPerfect)
          ─DOS UTILITIES
          │    └──chkdsk- Analyze Disk  (IBM/MS)
          ─EDUCATION
          │    └──The Playroom  (Broderbund Software)
          ─OPERATING
          │    └──Microsoft Windows  (Microsoft)
          ─PROGRAMMING
          │    └──Microsoft Linker  (Microsoft)
          ─UTILITIES

  ↵ Execute highlighted item               F10 commands  F1 help  ESC exit
```

Figure 13.1: The Application menu

Application menu commands

Menu	Description
XTree	Lists commands for getting help, executing a DOS command, and exiting the menu or XTreeGold.
Edit	Lists the commands which let you add, delete, modify, or rename a menu item; undo a change; and go into editing mode by selecting *Edit script*.
Options	Lists commands that let you change the way the menu is displayed.

Table 13.1: Application menu pull-down menus

In XTreePro Gold 1.0, available commands are displayed only at the bottom of the screen. The menu area is blank until you create a menu. To create a menu, you simply add new items to this empty menu. Follow the instructions in the next section, under "Adding and Modifying Menu Items."

The Application Menu

Select any item from this menu in one of the following ways:

- Move the highlight bar to the item by pressing the Up or Down Arrow, and then press Enter.
- Select the item by pointing to it with the mouse and double-clicking the left mouse button.

Selecting items from the menu

Adding and Modifying Menu Items

If you are using XTreePro Gold 1.0, skip to the section called "XTreePro Gold 1.0 Only."

XTreeGold 2.0 Only

You can change this Application menu on two levels. The first level includes changes that you'll see on the tree. The second level includes changes in the script, or access routine, for the application.

You can move, rename, or delete any item by selecting the item and then applying a command from the Edit pull-down menu. However, if you move or rename an item, the script associated with the item will not change.

The *script* is the batch file associated with an application. It is executed when you select the application from the Application menu. Category headers, shown in capital letters in Figure 13.1, have no scripts or batch files associated with them and cannot be executed. They are included to help organize the menu.

Item script

If you want to add a new item to the menu, first select the location for the new item. Then, select the *Add* command from the Edit pull-down menu. When you select *Add,* all items below the cursor move down, creating a new line at the location you selected. You can then type in the item.

Adding an item

You are now ready to work on the second level of the menu, the script associated with an item. Select the item you have just added (or any other item you want to modify). Then, select the *Edit script* command from the Edit pull-down menu. Once you are at this second level, the screen and pull-down menus change, and the commands are also displayed in the Edit command menu at the bottom of the screen (see Figure 13.2). You edit the script by selecting commands from the Edit pull-down menu or from the Edit command menu.

Modifying the menu in 2.0

Here's how to add a new item and write its script. If you want to modify the script for an existing item, simply highlight the item and start at #4 in the following exercise. If you want to add an item, *Reader Rabbit,* to the *Education* category, start at #1. You can substitute any program for *Reader Rabbit,* any directory for *Learning* and any category for *Education.*

1. With the Application menu open, highlight the first item under *Education* with the Up or Down Arrow or by clicking on it with the left mouse button.

2. Open the Edit pull-down menu and click the left mouse button on *Add item* or press A. You will see that a new line is ready at the selected location and the cursor is blinking.

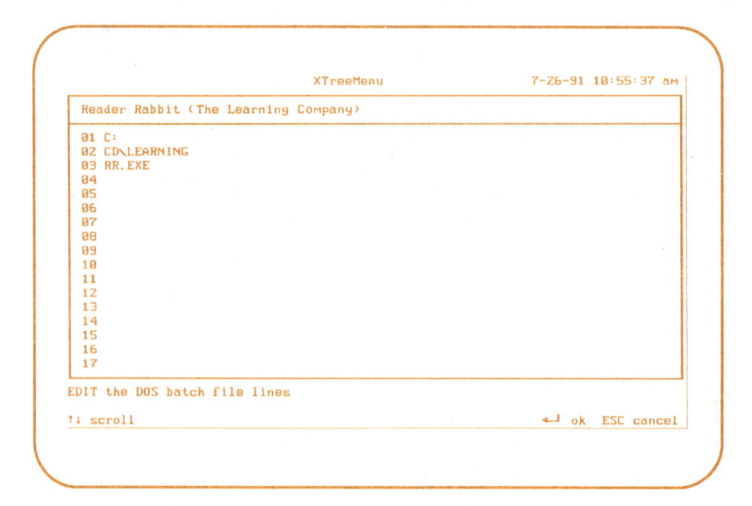

```
                           XTreeMenu            7-26-91 10:55:37 am
 Reader Rabbit (The Learning Company)
 01 C:
 02 CD\LEARNING
 03 RR.EXE
 04
 05
 06
 07
 08
 09
 10
 11
 12
 13
 14
 15
 16
 17
 EDIT the DOS batch file lines
 ↑↓ scroll                                       ↵ ok   ESC cancel
```

Figure 13.2: The Edit script screen

3. Type **Reader Rabbit (The Learning Company)** and press Enter or click the left mouse button on *ok*. The highlight bar is still on the item.

4. Open the Edit pull-down menu again and click the left mouse button on *Edit script* or press E. The Editing screen is now open.

5. Press Enter to begin editing the script at line 01, where you see the blinking cursor.

6. Type the script as though you were writing a batch file, using the Down Arrow instead of Enter to move to the next line. Type **C:** and press the Down Arrow, then type **CD \LEARNING** and press the Down Arrow, then type **RR.EXE** and press Enter or click the left mouse button on *ok* to complete your editing.

7. Now press Q or click the left mouse button on Quit in the command menu. If you want to execute the item, which is still highlighted, just press Enter or double-click on it with the left mouse button.

XTreePro Gold 1.0 Only

In XTreePro Gold 1.0, if you want to add a new item to the Application menu, first select a blank line by pointing and clicking the left mouse button or highlighting and pressing Enter. Then select *Edit* from the command menu. As soon as you select *Edit*, you are prompted for the name of the item. When you enter the item name, the cursor appears on line 01 of the editing screen, and you can type in the contents of the batch file.

Adding a menu item

If you want to edit an item, either to change its name or the contents of the batch file, just highlight the item and select the *Edit item* command to move to the editing screen.

Modifying an item in 1.0

Here's how to add a new item to the menu and write the batch file for it. To modify the batch file for an existing item, simply highlight the item and start at #4. If you wanted to add an item called *Reader Rabbit*, you would use the following procedure. Substitute any program for *Reader Rabbit* and any directory for *Learning*.

Modifying the menu

1. With the Application menu open, highlight the first line and press E or click the left mouse button on *Edit item.*

2. Type the item name, **Reader Rabbit,** and press Enter or click the left mouse button on *ok.*

3. Press E or click *Edit* to begin editing the batch file at the blinking cursor on line 01.

4. Type the batch file, using the Down Arrow instead of Enter to move to the next line, as follows. Type **C:** and press the Down Arrow, then type **CD \LEARNING** and press the Down Arrow. Finally, type **RR.EXE** and press the Down Arrow.

5. To complete your edit, press Enter on the blank line, then press Esc. If you want to execute the item, which is still highlighted, just press Enter or double-click on it with the left mouse button.

Organizing and Customizing the Menu Tree

The XTreeGold 2.0 Application menu looks like a directory tree and has similar expansion and contraction capabilities. If you think of the menu title as being like the root directory, and each category in upper case letters as a first level directory, then you can apply similar expand and collapse keystroke and mouse techniques to the menu.

The symbols in Table 13.2 indicate what lies beneath a menu item.

Symbol	Description
blank space	All menu items in that category are displayed.
+ (plus sign)	There are additional items and possibly additional categories beneath that category.

Table 13.2: Menu tree symbols

Expanding and Collapsing the Directory Tree Display

The quickest way to contract and restore the menu is to:

1. Place the mouse pointer to the left of the category title, making sure that the pointer is between the scroll bar and the tree.
2. Double-click the left mouse button. A plus sign appears.
3. Now place the mouse pointer in the same spot (it will be on the + this time) and double-click the left mouse button again. The display is restored and a blank space is inserted next to the item.

With the mouse

To contract and restore the menu with keystrokes:

1. Use the Arrow keys to highlight the category header.
2. Press F6. A plus sign appears.
3. Press F6 again. The display is restored and a blank space is inserted next to the item.

With keystrokes

To contract and restore the menu using the pull-down menu commands:

1. Use the Arrow keys to highlight the category header or point to it with the mouse and click the left mouse button.
2. Open the Options pull-down menu by clicking the left mouse button on *Options* or pressing F10.
3. Click the left mouse button on *Collapse branch* or press C. A plus sign appears.
4. Open the Options menu again and click the left mouse button on *Expand branch,* or press B. The display is restored and a blank space is inserted next to the item.

With pull-down menus

The Options menu also lists the accelerator keys for collapsing and expanding the menu.

Step 14

Launching Applications

In this step, you will learn how to use XTreeGold's Open commands to simultaneously start, or "launch," an application and open a file in the same application. The Open commands described in this step are available with both XTreeGold 1.0 and 2.0.

The Open Commands

Launching—or automatically starting—an application through a pre-established association with the selected file, is more convenient and quicker than starting the application and then loading the file. XTreeGold's launch capabilities are provided by the Open commands. To use these capabilities, you must:

1. Create a batch file for each application you will want to launch. This is a one-time task. The batch file is permanent and will be reused.

2. Select a data file to be loaded when you start the application, by positioning the highlight bar on the file (do not tag the file).

3. Select one of the Open commands. This starts the associated application for the selected data file.

The *Open (quick)* command on the File pull-down menu, or the *Open* command on the Standard file command menu, launches an application without changing the memory XTreeGold is currently using. The *Open (all memory)* command on the File pull-down menu, or the *Open* command on the Alt file command menu, launches an application and in the process minimizes the memory XTreeGold is currently using. The Open commands can be selected only when a File window is active.

Creating Batch Files With XTreeGold's Editor

For every application you want to launch with the Open command, you must create a batch file. You can create a batch file with any text editor or word processor that lets you save files in ASCII format. The batch file must meet the following criteria:

- The name of the batch file must be the same as the extension on the associated files. For instance, if you want to run the application Microsoft Word and open document files with the .WP extension, your batch file must be called WP.BAT.
- The batch file must be stored in the XTGOLD directory or in the alternate directory in which you installed XTreeGold.
- The batch file must contain the command needed to start the application, as well as a variable that uses the parameters shown in Table 14.1. The variable tells XTreeGold what file information to include in the batch file as it is executed.

Parameter	To insert the file's
%1	Path and name (C:\WORD\MEMOS\MEMO45.WP)
%2	Drive letter only (C)
%3	Path (\WORD\MEMOS)
%4	Name only (MEMO45)
%5	Extension only (WP)

Table 14.1: Batch file parameters

Creating the batch file

In the following example, you will use XTreeGold's edit command to create a batch file that selects a Microsoft Word document and launches Word at the same time. (You will find out more about the Edit command in Step 19.)

Launching Applications

1. Start with the Directory window active. Select the XTGOLD directory with the mouse or Arrow keys.
2. Press Alt-E or double-click the left mouse button on *DIR COMMANDS*. Click Edit to invoke the 1Word editor.
3. At the *Edit file* prompt, type **WP.BAT** and press Enter.
4. The 1Word screen appears with the cursor blinking. Type in the batch file as shown in Figure 14.1. Type **C:** and press Enter. Then, type **CD \WORD** and press Enter. Finally, type **WORD.EXE %1** and press Enter.
5. Press Esc to display the Quit command menu. *Save and Quit* is highlighted. Press Enter to confirm.

Now that you've written the batch file, you can apply the Open command to any Word files that have the .WP extension.

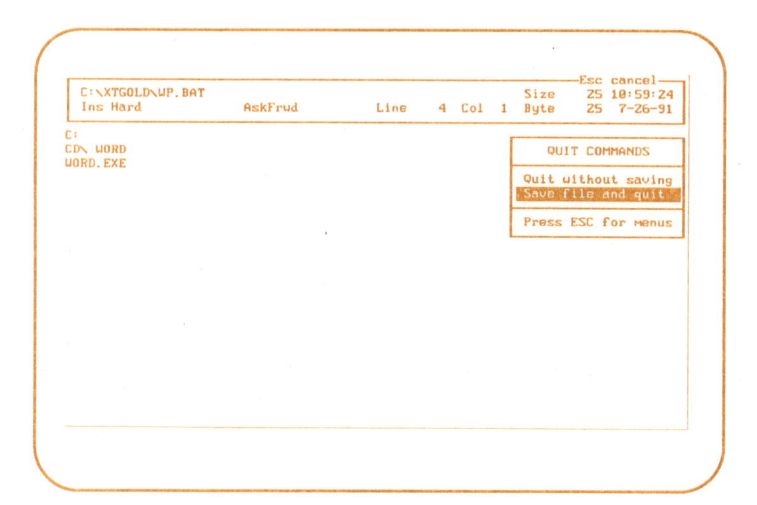

```
C:\XTGOLD\WP.BAT                                    Esc cancel
Ins Hard        AskFrud      Line   4 Col 1    Size   25 10:59:24
                                               Byte   25  7-26-91
C:
CD\ WORD                                    QUIT COMMANDS
WORD.EXE
                                         Quit without saving
                                         Save file and quit
                                         Press ESC for menus
```

Figure 14.1: The 1Word screen with the batch file written

Opening a Batch File in its Application

With any File window open, use the mouse or Arrow keys to select a file, then select one of the Open commands. XTreeGold will find the associated batch file.

1. Use the left mouse button or Arrow keys to highlight a file.
2. Open the File pull-down menu and click the left mouse button on *Open (all memory)* or press Alt-O.

If you hear a beep and nothing else happens XTreeGold can't open the selected file, because it can't locate the associated batch file. No error message is displayed on the screen if the Open command doesn't work. If you really have created the batch file, make sure it's named correctly and is in the right directory.

Step 15
Archiving Files

To make backup copies of files, use XTreeGold's Archive command rather than the copy commands. The Archive command compresses files so you will use fewer diskettes. Also use the Archive command to compress files for transfer via modem, to speed up the communications process, or to pack a larger amount of data onto a hard disk.

This step shows you how to use the options provided by the Archive command to compress and copy files. The command is available in XTreeGold 1.0 and 2.0. However, the newer version offers several additional options.

Zip and Arc Capabilities

With XTreeGold 2.0, the two archiving methods most commonly used for PCs are available:

- The Zip format, which is considered the most efficient for compressing files.

- The Arc format, which provides compatibility with other users and bulletin boards that use this format. It is slightly less efficient for file compression than the Zip format. (Only the Arc format is available in version 1.0.)

If you are archiving files for your own use and compatibility is not an issue, always use the Zip format to compress files into the smallest amount of disk space.

In addition to compressing files, the Archive command lets you:

- Add password protection to your archive files.
- Organize files within directories by preserving the original directory structure within the archive.
- Select one or more files to be included in an archive file.

- Add additional files to an archive file at any time in the future.
- Replace an older version of a file in an archive file with a more recent version, at any time in the future.

To compress files anywhere on the current volume to an archive file you will:

Archiving files

1. Tag all the files.
2. Display them in the most suitable File window.
3. Select the Archive files command to create the archive file in the directory of your choice.

Creating Zip and Arc Files

To archive all tagged files in any File window to a destination of your choice, use any of the following methods:

- Open the Tagged pull-down menu and click the left mouse button on *Zip and Arc,* or press Z.
- Click the left mouse button on *FILE COMMANDS* and then on *archive files* in the command menu.
- Press Ctrl-F5.

Selecting the Zip or Arc format

When you have selected the *archive files* command, you are prompted for the file destination and file name. At this point, you can determine whether you want to archive your files in the Zip or Arc format. XTreeGold 2.0 will use the Zip format unless you type in a file name with the extension **.ARC**. If you do not type in the .ARC extension, the .ZIP extension is added automatically, and the Zip format is used for archiving. If you type in any other extension, for example, **.BAK**, that extension is used for the archived file, which is archived in Zip format. The Zip and Arc options are not shown in the prompt line.

Selecting a destination

When you select the *Archive files* command, the ↑ *history* option appears in the prompt line, but the *F2 point* option does not.

Archiving Files

However, at the prompt, you can type in another destination directory for the archive file.

When you have entered a name and destination for the archive file, the additional archiving options are displayed. These options, which are described in Table 15.1, vary according to whether you have selected the Zip or Arc format.

Archiving options

Option	Description
Paths	Archives files with their directory structure (Zip only).
Compatibility	Lets you choose between the Arc format and XTree format. The XTree format archives files with their directory structure (Arc only).
Encryption	Lets you give your archive file a password of up to 32 characters.
Method	For an existing archive file, Method lets you (1) add all tagged files unconditionally (archive), (2) add only those files that replace archived files of the same name and older date (freshen), (3) both "freshen" previously archived files and archive other tagged files for the first time (update).
Speed/size	Lets you indicate whether faster archiving speed or smaller archive file size should be the determining factor in the method XTreeGold uses (Zip only).

Table 15.1: Archiving options

This practice session uses the Zip format to archive all files in a directory and create an archive file in another directory.

1. Start with the Directory window active. Select the directory you want to back up, using the left mouse button or Arrow keys.

2. Press T or open the Tag pull-down menu and click the left mouse button on *Directory files*.

3. Highlight the directory again, and press Enter or click ↵ *files* in the command menu.

4. Press Ctrl-F5 or open the Tagged pull-down menu and click the left mouse button on *Zip and Arc*.

5. Type in the destination directory and file name with or without an extension—for example, **\ARCHIVE\ARC2**—and press Enter.

6. From the options menu at the bottom of the screen, change any options displayed by pressing the highlighted letter or clicking the left mouse button on the option. For example, change the default from *size* to *speed* by pressing S.

7. Press Enter or click *ok* in the prompt line to archive the tagged files.

8. When the archiving process has been completed, the File window is still active. Press Ctrl-U to untag all the files, then press Esc to return to the Directory window.

9. Select the directory ARCHIVE in which you created the archive file, with the left mouse button or Arrow keys. You'll see the file ARC1.ZIP in the File window. If you want to copy this file to a diskette, simply highlight it in the File window and select the *Copy* command.

For more information on the Copy command, see Step 6.

Updating a Zip or Arc File

At some point, you will probably want either to modify files in or add files to this archive file. This is quicker and more practical than creating new archive files and discarding the old ones.

Updating an archive

In this practice session, you will learn how to update the archive file for a directory by adding the new files and replacing older version of existing files.

Archiving Files

1. Start with the Directory window active. Using the left mouse button or Arrow keys, select the directory whose archive file you are updating.
2. Press T or open the Tag pull-down menu and click the left mouse button on *Directory files.*
3. Highlight the directory again. Press Enter or click ↵ *files* in the command menu.
4. Press Ctrl-F5, or open the Tagged pull-down menu and click the left mouse button on *Zip and Arc.*
5. Press the Up Arrow or click *history,* and select the archive file from the history window. Highlight **\ARCHIVE\ARC2.ZIP** with the Up Arrow and press Enter, or click the left mouse button on the file and press Enter.
6. Press Enter or click *ok* to confirm the destination and file name shown in the prompt line.
7. In the options menu at the bottom of the screen, change any options displayed by pressing the highlighted letter or clicking the left mouse button on the option. Change the method to *update* by pressing M or clicking *Method.* This adds new files and replaces less recent files in the archive.
8. Press Enter or click *ok* in the prompt line to archive the tagged files.
9. When the archiving process has been completed, the File window is still active. Press Ctrl-U to untag all the files.

Step 16

Extracting Archived Files

XTreeGold's extract capabilities enable you to extract any or all files from an archive file that:

- You created yourself with XTreeGold.
- Was provided to you, archived in either Zip or Arc format, on diskette or by modem.
- You have downloaded from a bulletin board.

This step shows you how to use the options provided by the *Open archive* command to extract files. The command is available in XTreeGold 1.0 and 2.0. However, files archived with the Zip format can only be handled by version 2.0.

Opening a Zip or Arc file

To extract the contents of an archive file, select the file using the highlight bar in any File window. Then, select the *Open Zip and Arc* command from the File pull-down menu or the *Open archive* command from the Alt file command menu. The command names are different, but the commands are functionally the same. You can only open one archive file at a time; there is no command to open all tagged archive files.

Use the left mouse button or Arrow keys to highlight a file. Then, choose any of the following techniques to open an Archive window.

- Open the File pull-down menu and click the left mouse button on *Open Zip and Arc* or press Z.
- Double-click on *FILE COMMANDS*. Then, double-click on *open archive* in the command menu.
- Press Alt-F5.

Opening an archive

Moving Around the Archive Windows

When you select the *Open archive* command, the window that XTreeGold opens depends on the structure and content of the archive file you selected. Either a Directory or a File window may open. Either window may be labeled an ARC window or ZIP window. If the directory structure of the files was copied into the archive when the archive was created, then an archive (Arc or Zip) Directory window is opened. If the directory structure was not created, an archive (Arc or Zip) File window will always be opened.

The main display for the Zip Directory window looks like a normal Directory window, but the commands and statistics boxes are different, as shown in Figure 16.1.

The main display for the Arc File window looks like the Expanded file window, though there are fewer commands and some differences in the statistics boxes, as shown in Figure 16.2.

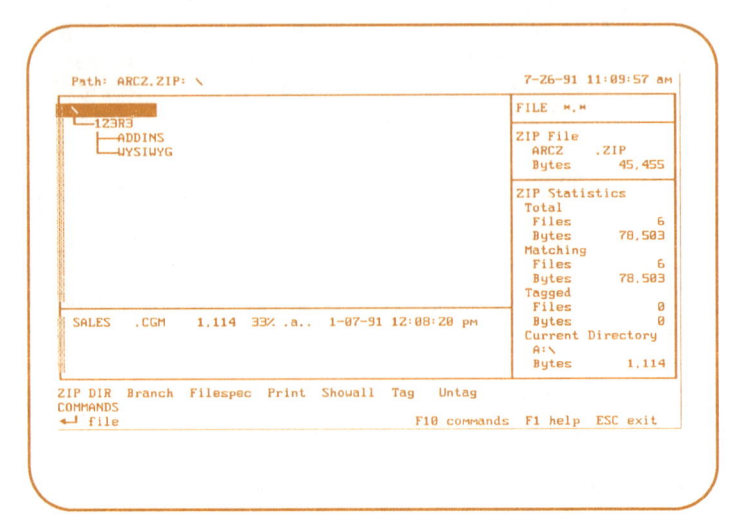

```
Path: ARCZ.ZIP: \                           7-26-91 11:09:57 am
                                       FILE  *.*
   └─123R3
      ├─ADDINS                         ZIP File
      └─WYSIWYG                           ARCZ    .ZIP
                                          Bytes        45,455

                                       ZIP Statistics
                                       Total
                                          Files             6
                                          Bytes        78,503
                                       Matching
                                          Files             6
                                          Bytes        78,503
                                       Tagged
                                          Files             0
   SALES    .CGM   1,114  33% .a..  1-07-91 12:08:20 pm    Bytes             0
                                       Current Directory
                                       A:\
                                          Bytes         1,114

ZIP DIR  Branch  Filespec  Print  Showall  Tag  Untag
COMMANDS
 ↵ file                              F10 commands  F1 help  ESC exit
```

Figure 16.1: Zip Directory window

Extracting Archived Files

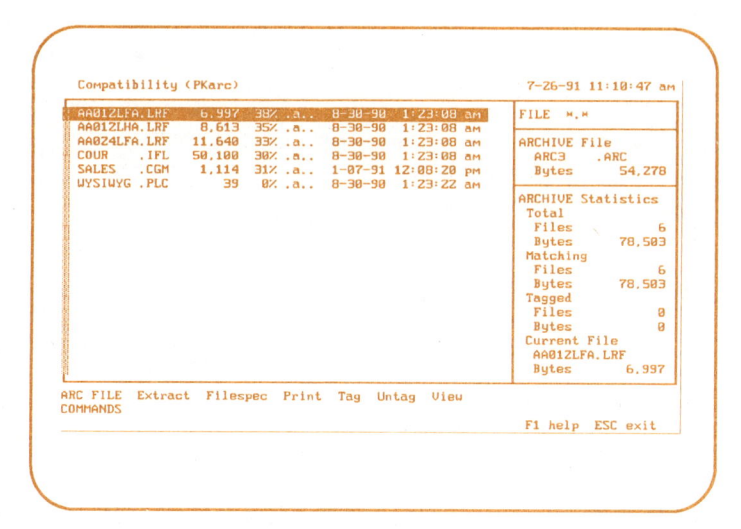

```
Compatibility (PKarc)                           7-26-91 11:10:47 am

AA01ZLFA.LRF    6,997  38% .a..  8-30-90  1:23:08 am   FILE  *.*
AA01ZLHA.LRF    8,613  35% .a..  8-30-90  1:23:08 am
AA0Z4LFA.LRF   11,640  33% .a..  8-30-90  1:23:08 am   ARCHIVE File
COUR    .IFL   50,100  30% .a..  8-30-90  1:23:08 am     ARC3    .ARC
SALES   .CGM    1,114  31% .a..  1-07-91 12:08:20 pm     Bytes     54,278
WYSIWYG .PLC       39   0% .a..  8-30-90  1:23:22 am
                                                       ARCHIVE Statistics
                                                       Total
                                                         Files           6
                                                         Bytes      78,503
                                                       Matching
                                                         Files           6
                                                         Bytes      78,503
                                                       Tagged
                                                         Files           0
                                                         Bytes           0
                                                       Current File
                                                         AA01ZLFA.LRF
                                                         Bytes       6,997

ARC FILE   Extract  Filespec  Print  Tag  Untag  View
COMMANDS
                                                       F1 help   ESC exit
```

Figure 16.2: Arc file window

A percentage is displayed for each file listed in the File window. This percentage is the amount the archived file has been compressed compared to the size of the original file. The byte size of the original file is shown next to the percentage.

To extract archive files, select the most suitable File window, then select the file(s) you want to extract from the archive.

Using the Archive Menus

Only the commands displayed in the command and pull-down menus can be applied while an Archive window is active. These pull-down menus contain the commands listed in Tables 16.1 and 16.2.

Menu	Description
XTree	Lists commands for getting help and exiting the Archive window. These commands are also available from the Standard Archive menu.

Archive directory commands

Table 16.1: Archive directory window pull-down menus

Menu	Description
Volume	Lists the *Print* command, which prints a catalog of files in the archive. The *Print* command is also available from the Standard Archive menu.
Tag	Lists the Standard, Ctrl, Alt, Tag, and Untag commands available in the Directory window.
Window	Lists commands for choosing another window or changing the way file information is displayed. These commands are also available from the Standard, Ctrl, or Alt Archive menus.

Table 16.1: *Archive directory window pull-down menus (continued)*

Archive file commands

Menu	Description
XTree	Lists commands for getting help and exiting the Archive window. These commands are also available from the Standard Archive menu.
File	Lists the *Extract, Print,* and *View* commands, which act on a selected file in the archive. These commands are also available from the Standard Archive menu.
Tagged	Lists the *Extract files* and *Extract with paths* commands, which act on tagged files. These commands are available from the Ctrl and Alt menus.
Tag	Lists the Standard, Ctrl, Alt, Tag, and Untag commands available in the File window.
Window	Lists commands for changing the way file information is displayed. These commands are also available from the Standard, Ctrl, or Alt Archive menus.

Table 16.2: *Archive file window pull-down menus*

Displaying the Contents of an Archive File

You can view the contents of an archive file whether the Archive file window or Archive directory window is opened first. The Archive file window displays a list of files in the archive. You can select a file in the list and display it in the View window without extracting it. You can only select and view one file at a time in the View window. From the Archive file window:

1. Use the left mouse button or Arrow keys to highlight a file.
2. Select *View* from the File pull-down menu or command menu.

Viewing a file

From the Archive directory window, simply select the most suitable File window to look at a list of the files. The Small, Expanded, Branch, and Showall file windows are all available.

Extracting Files From an Archive

This practice session shows you how to extract files from an archive file.

1. Use the left mouse button or Arrow keys to select the archive file you want to open.
2. Press Alt-F5, or open the File pull-down menu and click the left mouse button on *Open Zip and Arc*.
3. You want the Archive file window to be active. If the Directory window is opened by XTreeGold, select *Showall* from the Window pull-down menu or from the command menu.
4. In the Archive file window, tag all the files you want to extract by highlighting a file and pressing T or clicking on it with the right mouse button. Repeat the procedure for each file. To tag all the files in the window, press Ctrl-Tag or open the tag pull-down menu and click the left mouse button on *All in window*.

5. Once the files are tagged, you can extract them. To extract them and preserve their directory structure, either press Alt-E or open the Tagged pull-down menu and click the left mouse button on *Extract with paths*.

6. At the *filename* prompt, press Enter or click *ok* in the prompt line to retain the original file names.

7. At the destination prompt, press F2 or click the left mouse button on *point* in the prompt line to open the Destination directory window. Then highlight the destination for the files. Press Enter or click on *ok* to confirm the destination shown.

8. This prompt asks whether or not you want to replace existing files. Type N or click *No* if you want to be prompted before a file is copied over.

9. The final prompt asks for a password, regardless of whether the archive file was password protected. Either type the password and press Enter or, if the file is not password protected, just press Enter.

10. The tagged files are extracted into the directory you selected. Press Esc twice, or open the XTree pull-down menu and click the left mouse button on *Quit to Gold* to return to the File window.

Step 17

Comparing Files

XTreeGold provides two commands for comparing files:

- The Directory window *Compare* command, which compares the file list in one directory with the file list in another directory.

- The File window *Compare* command, which compares files listed in the current File window.

This step shows you how to use each of these commands. These commands are only available in XTreeGold 2.0.

Compare Capabilities and Options

You can use XTreeGold's Compare commands to:

- Determine whether or not the files in a directory match its backup directory on another disk or volume.

- Identify any duplicate files located across all directories in a branch, in a volume, or on all logged disks.

- Locate all versions of files in a branch, on a volume, or on all logged disks, and display the most recent version.

- Quickly list, or list and tag, files that are unique.

You can use these capabilities to help organize and clean up your own hard disk, as well as those of others in your organization for which you are responsible. The Compare commands enable you to see where and how files have become disorganized. This can easily happen when several people are sharing a system, or when novice users have been inadvertently saving copies of files in multiple directories.

When the Directory window is active, choosing the *Compare* command provides you with a set of options for comparing one directory to another. Table 17.1 describes these options. When you

Directory window Compare command

select one or more options, XTreeGold tags files in the first directory that satisfy the conditions of the comparison. The options are not mutually exclusive.

Option	Description
Identical	Tags each file that has an exact match in the second directory in name, size, attributes, and date.
Unique	Tags each file that does not exist in the second directory, with the same file name.
Newer	Compares two files with the same name, and if the file in the first directory is newer, tags it.
Older	Compares two files with the same name, and if the file in the first directory is older, tags it.

Table 17.1: *Directory window* **Compare** *command options*

File window Compare command

When a File window is active, choosing the *Compare* command provides you with a set of options for making comparisons among all the files in the window. Table 17.2 describes these options. When you have selected an option or options, XTreeGold makes the comparison, then displays the files that match the options you selected. XTreeGold does not tag the files; but, when the comparison is finished, the File window contains only the files that match your selected criteria. The File window *Compare* command only appears when a Branch, Showall, or Global file window is active.

Option	Description
Duplicate name	Lists each file that has an exact match in file name in the window.
Unique name	Lists each file that is unique in name in the window.

Table 17.2: *File window* **Compare** *command options*

Option	Description
Identical dates	Used with Duplicate, compares all files with the same name, and lists all files that also have the same date.
Newest date	Used with Duplicate, compares all files with the same name, and lists the duplicate file with the newest date.
Oldest date	Used with Duplicate name, compares all files with the same name, and lists the duplicate file with the oldest date.
Scope	Used only when you're working in the Global window, lets you decide whether to compare all files or compare files using their path information as well.

Table 17.2: File window **Compare** *command options (continued)*

Comparing Files in One Directory With Another

Before selecting the *Compare* command, highlight the directory (the first directory) in which you want to find points of comparison to another directory (the second directory). The second directory can be on any disk or volume. Select the *Compare* command from the Directory pull-down menu or the Standard directory command menu.

To compare files in two directories on the same volume, follow these steps.

1. Use the left mouse button or Arrow keys to highlight the first directory, which will eventually contain tagged files.
2. Open the Directory pull-down menu and click the left mouse button on *Compare*, or press C. Enter the path and name of the second directory at the prompt, as shown in Figure 17.1.

Up & Running with XTreeGold 2

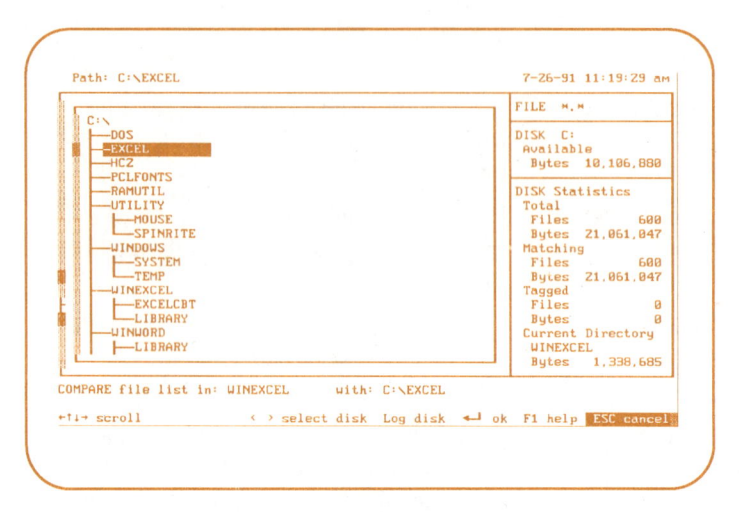

[Screenshot of XTreeGold directory compare screen showing path C:\EXCEL with directory tree and disk statistics]

Figure 17.1: Entering the Directory compare path

When you select the *Compare* command, the ↑ *history* and the *F2 point* options appear in the prompt line.

3. Press F2 to display the Destination directory window. Then select the second directory with the left mouse button or arrow keys.

4. Press Enter or click *ok* in the prompt line to confirm the destination. Now choose from the options, as shown in Figure 17.2. Options are always displayed in the same way, regardless of your previous selections.

5. To find all identical files contained in both directories, press I or click the left mouse button on *Identical,* changing it to read *Identical (yes).* Then, deselect Unique, Newer, and Older by clicking on them, or by pressing the highlighted letter key, so that *(no)* appears following each of these options.

6. Press Enter or click *ok* in the prompt line to begin the compare operation.

Comparing Files **111**

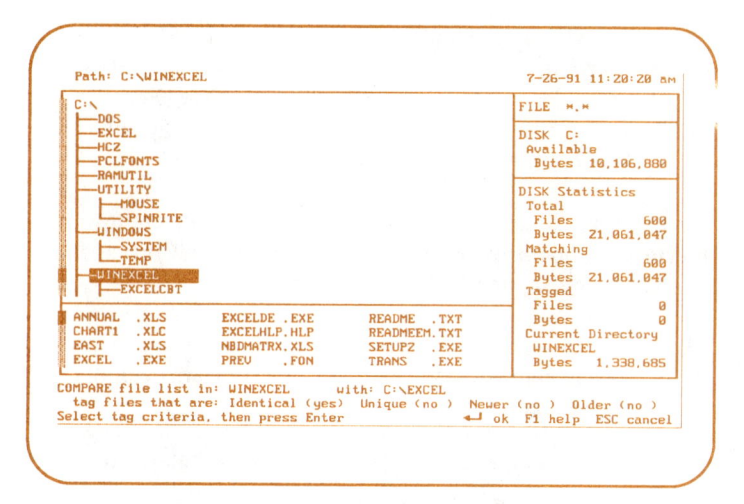

```
Path: C:\WINEXCEL                          7-26-91 11:20:20 am
C:\                                        FILE  *.*
 ├─DOS
 ├─EXCEL                                   DISK  C:
 ├─HCZ                                     Available
 ├─PCLFONTS                                  Bytes      10,106,880
 ├─RAMUTIL
 ├─UTILITY                                 DISK Statistics
 │  ├─MOUSE                                Total
 │  └─SPINRITE                              Files                600
 ├─WINDOWS                                  Bytes         21,061,047
 │  ├─SYSTEM                               Matching
 │  └─TEMP                                  Files                600
 ├─WINEXCEL                                 Bytes         21,061,047
 │  └─EXCELCBT                             Tagged
                                            Files                  0
 ANNUAL  .XLS    EXCELDE .EXE   README  .TXT   Bytes              0
 CHART1  .XLC   EXCELHLP.HLP   READMEEM.TXT
 EAST    .XLS   NBDMATRX.XLS   SETUP2  .EXE   Current Directory
 EXCEL   .EXE   PREV    .FON   TRANS   .EXE   WINEXCEL
                                              Bytes       1,338,685
 COMPARE file list in: WINEXCEL   with: C:\EXCEL
   tag files that are: Identical (yes)  Unique (no )  Newer (no )  Older (no )
 Select tag criteria, then press Enter          ↵ ok  F1 help  ESC cancel
```

Figure 17.2: Choosing the Directory compare options

When the operation is completed, all identical files are tagged in the first directory. You can now use any operation with them by selecting the File window.

Comparing Files Across Directories

The *Compare* command on the Alt file command menu compares all files in a Branch, Showall, or Global file window and displays only those that meet your specifications. This command is not listed on any pull-down menu.

The *Compare* command in the Showall window compares all files on the current volume.

In the Showall file window

Use the following procedure to compare all files on the current volume and identify all those with duplicate names, regardless of dates.

1. Start with the Directory window active and select the Showall file window by pressing S or clicking the left mouse button on *Showall* in the command menu.

112 *Up & Running with XTreeGold 2*

2. Press Alt-F4, or double-click on the words *FILE COMMANDS* in the lower left of the screen and then click on *compare*. Now choose from the options as shown in Figure 17.3. These options are displayed in this way only when the Branch or Showall window is active.

Notice that the options are not marked *yes* or *no*. By contrast, the Directory compare command options are marked *yes* and *no*. Choose only one option from those shown.

3. Select all duplicate files by pressing D or clicking *Duplicate*. No confirmation is needed. The compare operation starts immediately.

When the comparison is completed, only the duplicate files are displayed in the Showall file window. You can now use any operation with the files, including tagging.

In the Branch file window

The compare command in the Branch file window compares all files in any branch. Use the same technique described in the previous action, except choose the Branch window in #1.

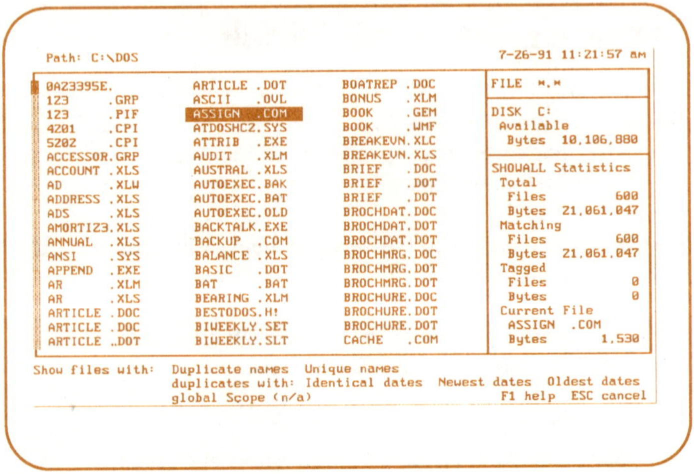

Figure 17.3: Choosing the File compare options

Comparing Files Across Volumes

When you use Compare in the Global file window to compare files in two or more logged disks, the Scope option becomes active. Except for the addition of the Scope option, the Compare command works in the Global file window as it does in the Branch or Showall file windows. The Scope option lets you further specify where you want XTreeGold to search in comparing files.

In the Global file window

Option	Description
all	Files will be compared on all logged drives and in all directories.
across drives	Files on different disks or volumes will be listed.
matching paths	Only files with matching paths (on different disks or volumes) will be listed.

Table 17.3: Global file window Scope options

The following procedure compares all files on all logged volumes and identifies all with duplicate names across drives.

1. Start with the Directory window active and select the Global file window by pressing G or clicking *Global* in the command menu.

2. Press Alt-F4 or double-click on the words *FILE COMMANDS* in the lower left of the screen and then click on *compare*. Now choose from the options shown. You will notice that the Scope option is set to the default *(matching paths)*.

3. First select the scope option, all, by pressing S until you see *Scope (all)* or by clicking Scope one or two times.

4. Select all duplicate files by pressing D or clicking on *Duplicate*. No confirmation is needed. The compare operation starts immediately.

When completed, all duplicate files and only duplicate files on different disks or volumes are displayed in the Global file window. You can now perform any operation you wish on them, including tagging them.

Step 18

Undeleting Files

This step shows you how to use the *Oops!* command to undelete—or recover—deleted files. The *Oops!* command is only available in XTreeGold 2.0.

What You Can Do with *Oops!*

XTreeGold's Undelete command, called *Oops!*, lets you undelete files, one at a time, that meet certain criteria. To be recovered, files:

- Must not be in conflict with other files.
- Must not have been written over since they were deleted.
- Must not have been obscured by XTreeGold's *Wash disk* command or disk optimizer since they were deleted.

Even if files meet these conditions, there is no guarantee that the undelete process will work. However, there is a good chance it will work. So, if you have deleted files you need, you should use the *Oops!* command to try to recover them.

To undelete a file, first select the directory in which the file was located. Select the *Oops!* command from the Directory pull-down menu or the Standard directory command menu. You can't open this window if you have selected a directory that does not contain deleted files, or that is on a network or substitute volume. Instead, an error message is displayed in the prompt line.

What's in the Undelete Window

By selecting *Oops!*, you open the Undelete window, shown in Figure 18.1. The Undelete window lists all the deleted files that may be recoverable.

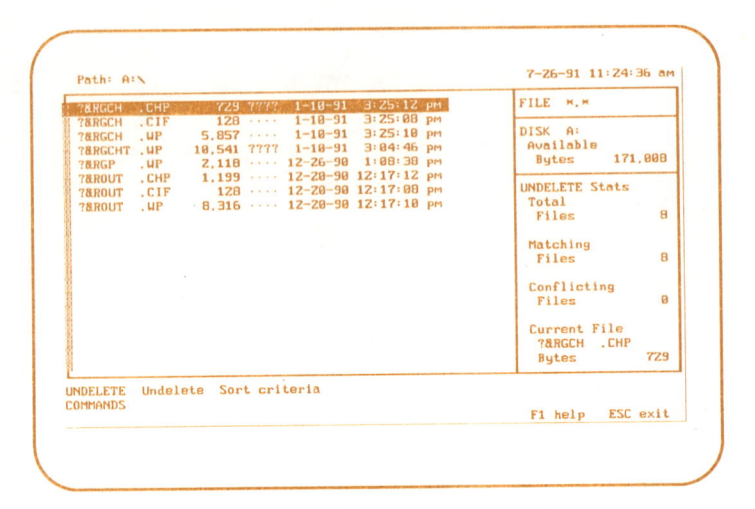

Figure 18.1: The Undelete file window

In this window, a one-column format is used for the file display. Because the first character in a file name is always erased when a file is deleted, XTreeGold cannot display it. A question mark is displayed instead. And no matter what file specification you were using when you selected *Oops!*, the *.* file specification is used in this window. However, your current sort order is used.

File attributes are not displayed. In their place you may see four question marks. These tell you the file is a conflicting file, one which you may not be able to undelete. Files are in conflict if, when they are undeleted, they would occupy the same physical disk space as would another deleted file.

The Statistics box does not give the byte size for the total or matching files, but does for the current file. The size of the current file is the amount of disk space it occupied before it was deleted.

Moving around the Undelete Window

You may not tag files in the Undelete window or undelete multiple files. You must select one file at a time to be undeleted, using one of the following techniques:

- Highlight a file with the Arrow keys.
- Point to the file and click the left mouse button.

Only four choices are displayed in the Undelete command menu at the bottom of the screen. These are described in Table 18.1. There are no Undelete pull-down menus.

Using the Undelete Menu

Command	Description
Undelete	Lets you undelete the selected file.
Sort criteria	Lets you change the way files are sorted in the Undelete window. Allows you to sort files by name, date, extension, and size.
Help	Immediately displays the *Oops!* command help screen.
Exit	Returns you to the Directory window with the current directory highlighted.

Table 18.1: Undelete window commands

Undeleting a File

To undelete a file:

1. Select the directory in which the file was located before it was deleted.
2. Select the *Oops!* command.
3. If the file name is displayed in the Undelete window (with a question mark as the first character), select the file.
4. Select the *Undelete* command.

This practice session shows how you can undelete a file from any directory.

1. Select the directory that contains the deleted file, using the left mouse button or Arrow keys.

2. Press O or open the Directory pull-down menu and click *Oops!*.

3. In the Undelete window, select the file you want to undelete, using the left mouse button or Arrow keys.

4. To undelete it, press U or click *Undelete*.

5. At the *filename* prompt, type in the original file name or any file name that is not duplicated in the current directory. Because files are always undeleted to their original directories, you will not be prompted for a destination. When you type the name and press Enter, XTreeGold starts the undelete process. A message in the prompt line tells you whether or not the file has been restored.

When the restore attempt is complete, XTreeGold updates the list of files in the Undelete window. Files that were in conflict with the file you just undeleted are no longer on the list. They can no longer be recovered. You cannot predict how undeleting a file in conflict will be resolved.

When you finish undeleting your files, check to make sure they have been restored completely and correctly. Return to the File window and either use the *View* command to browse through the contents (see Step 11) or open the file in its application (see Step 14). If you have restored many files in a directory, open the Autoview window for that directory (see Step 10).

Step 19

Editing Files

This step shows you how to use the Edit command to edit a text file. XTreeGold's editing capabilities are available in both versions 1.0 and 2.0.

Editing with the 1Word Text Editor

One of XTreeGold's commands opens a text editor that lets you create and modify text files conveniently, without returning to your word processing program. You can use the editing capabilities for everything from writing and editing batch files to creating memos, letters, or even larger documents.

Most people have a word processing program that they are proficient in and happy with. XTreeGold's editing command gives you a needed tool to use in file management tasks. Once you try it, you may find it's the best editor for many of your routine tasks.

To edit a file when a File window is open, first select the file and then select the *Edit* command. To edit a file when the Directory window is open, first select the directory in which the file is located and then select the *Edit* command. Select the *Edit* command from the File pull-down menu, the Standard directory, or Standard File command menu.

Even though the *Edit* command is not displayed on the Standard directory command menu, you can select it by pressing E. The *Edit* command is displayed on the Alt directory command menu, but you need not select it from that menu.

If you select the *Edit* command with a File window open, the current file appears in the prompt line. If you select *Edit* with the Directory window open, no file name appears in the prompt line. After selecting *Edit,* you always have the option of typing in the name of a new or existing file. Or, using the ↑ *history* option, which is always displayed, you can enter at the prompt the name of any file displayed in the history window To easily create a new file:

Creating a new file

1. Start with the Directory window active and select, using the left mouse button or Arrow keys, the directory in which you want to create a new file.
2. Press E or open the File pull-down menu and click on *Edit*.
3. At the *EDIT file* prompt, type the name of the new file, and press Enter.

To easily edit an existing file:

Editing an existing file

1. Start with the File window active and use the left mouse button or pointer to select the File that you want to edit.
2. Press E, or open the File pull-down menu and click on *Edit*.
3. At the *EDIT file* prompt, press Enter. If you have selected the wrong file, press Backspace to delete the file name shown and type any other filename or select one from the history.

The 1Word window (Figure 19.1) opens and, if you selected an existing file, that file will be displayed in the window. The mouse becomes inactive when you start 1Word and remains so until you return to XTreeGold.

The 1Word Status Box

The status box always appears when you enter editing mode.

In the top line of the status box, you will see:

- The path and name of the file you are editing
- The size of the file, in bytes
- The current time

Editing Files 121

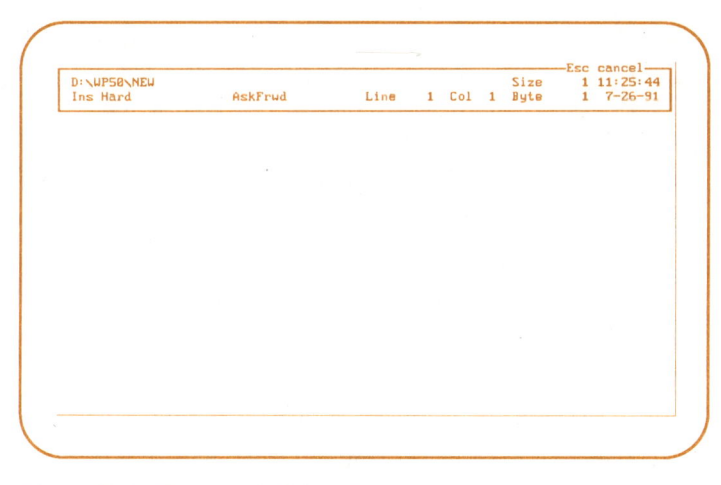

```
┌─────────────────────────────────────────────────Esc cancel─┐
│ D:\WP50\NEW                              Size    1 11:25:44│
│ Ins Hard         AskFrwd      Line  1 Col 1 Byte 1 7-26-91 │
│                                                            │
│                                                            │
│                                                            │
│                                                            │
│                                                            │
│                                                            │
└────────────────────────────────────────────────────────────┘
```

Figure 19.1: The 1Word editing window

In the bottom line of the status box, you'll see:

- *Ins* or *Ovr*, to indicate whether you are in insert or overwrite mode
- *Hard*, *Soft*, or *User*, to indicate how the tabs are currently set
- *Ask*, to indicate that Search and Replace mode is currently set to ask first
- *Frwd* or *Back* to indicate the Search direction currently set
- The current location of the cursor by line, column, and byte number. This will change as you edit.
- The current date

Other items you may see in the bottom line of the status box include:

- *Cap* or *Num*, if the Caps lock or Number lock is turned on at any time
- *Wrap*, if you turn on automatic word wrap

- *Case*, if you select case sensitivity in Search operations
- *Word*, if you select full-word sensitivity in Search operations

This status box is displayed whenever 1Word's menus are not displayed.

Getting help

Although it is not displayed in the Status box, the F1 help key is available any time the Status box is displayed.

Using 1Word's Menus

With 1Word, you can either rely primarily on Ctrl keys to select commands, or select commands from menus. If you are familiar with Wordstar, the similarities between 1Word and Wordstar commands make 1Word especially easy to learn. Otherwise, work with the menus for awhile. The Menu commands are well-organized and easy to locate.

Displaying the menus

Press Ctrl-U to display 1Word's menus. The menu shown in Figure 19.2 appears in place of the Status box.

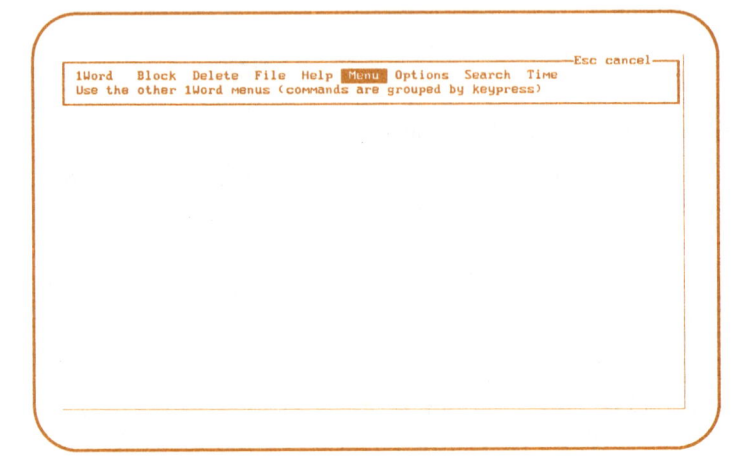

```
┌─────────────────────────────────────────── Esc cancel ──┐
│ 1Word   Block   Delete   File   Help  Menu  Options  Search  Time │
│ Use the other 1Word menus (commands are grouped by keypress)     │
│                                                                    │
│                                                                    │
└────────────────────────────────────────────────────────────────────┘
```

Figure 19.2: The 1Word command menu

From this menu, you can select another menu, a command, or help. (Pressing F1 only displays help when the Status box is displayed.) Table 19.1 describes the many functions available from the 1Word command menu.

To select a menu item, use the Right or Left arrow to highlight it, and press Enter.

Selecting a menu item

Menu item	Description
Block	Displays a menu with the commands for marking and manipulating blocks of text.
Delete	Displays a menu with the commands for deleting characters, words, lines, and blocks.
File	Displays a menu with the commands for importing files, saving files, printing files, and exiting to XTreeGold.
Help	Accesses the help screens.
Menu	Displays a menu from which all 1Word commands are available, grouped alphabetically.
Options	Displays a menu with the commands for changing the Insert, Word wrap, and Tab modes, and for quickly moving to any line.
Search	Displays a menu with the commands and options for searching and replacing text.
Time	Immediately inserts the current date and time at the cursor.

Table 19.1: 1Word menu items

Let's begin to create a brief "to do" list, relying on the menus for command help. Use the sample or make a useful list for yourself.

Creating a new document

1. Go back to the directions for creating a new file, if necessary. When you have created a new file, and while the Status box is displayed, press Ctrl-U to display the 1Word menu.
2. Now press the Right Arrow until the word *Time* is highlighted and press Enter. You have inserted the date and time at the top of today's list.
3. Press Ctrl-U again, then highlight Options and press Enter.
4. Highlight *Word wrap on/off* and press Enter to turn word wrap on in your document. You will notice that the word *Wrap* is now displayed in the Status box.

Entering and Editing text

Entering text

Now type in the first four items on the list, as shown:

1. Press Enter to end the line. Press Enter again to leave a line blank.
2. Now type the following items, pressing Enter at the end of each line.

   ```
   Item 1. Return all yesterday's unanswered
   phone calls.
   Item 2. Schedule 15-minute meeting to
   tell staff I'll be purchasing XTreeGold
   for them and reorganizing their hard
   disks with it.
   Item 3. Prepare to handle expected
   objections from staff during meeting.
   Item 4. Complete Step 20 and change the
   XTreeGold default configurations to suit
   me.
   ```

Obviously, entering text is very straightforward. Simple editing tasks are also easy.

Editing text

Now make some quick changes to your list. Use the Arrow keys to move around in the file quickly during editing.

Editing Files 125

1. Add a new item 4. Use the Arrow keys to move the cursor to the end of item 3 (following the period) and press Enter. Because you are in Insert mode, this adds a new line.

2. Now type:

   `Item 4. Archive outdated files on my disk with the Zip and Arc command.`

   Don't press Enter at the end of this sentence.

3. Now change the second item 4 to item 5. Press Insert to enter Overwrite mode. *Ovr* appears in the Status box. Press the Down Arrow, then Home, to move the cursor to the second item 4, and type **5**.

4. Now go back up to item 2 and change the 15-minute meeting to a 30-minute meeting. Press the Up Arrow to move to the line and the Right Arrow to move to the 1. Now type **30**. Pressing Insert again returns you from Overwrite to Insert mode.

The keys and commands you will use most for editing are shown in Table 19.2.

Editing keys

Keys	Description
Backspace	Deletes one character to the left of the cursor.
Delete	Deletes the character at the cursor location.
Insert	Toggles insert and overwrite modes.
Ctrl-T	Deletes the entire word in which the cursor is currently located.
Ctrl-Y	Deletes the entire line in which the cursor is currently located.
Ctrl-QY	Deletes all characters from the current cursor location to the end of the line.

Table 19.2: 1Word editing commands

Editing blocks

Use the Block Commands menu to edit blocks of text. Press Ctrl-U and then select *Block* to display the Block Commands menu (Figure 19.3).

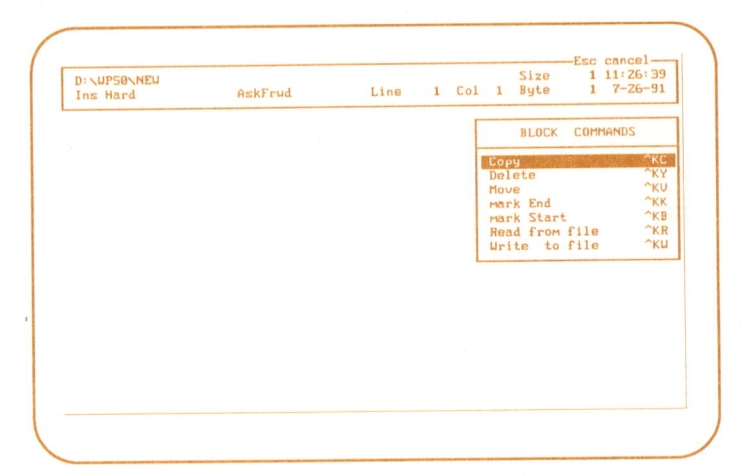

```
┌─────────────────────────────────────────────Esc cancel─┐
│ D:\WP50\NEW                           Size   1 11:26:39│
│ Ins Hard        AskFrud       Line 1 Col 1 Byte 1 7-26-91│
│                                     ┌─BLOCK COMMANDS──┐│
│                                     │ Copy         ^KC││
│                                     │ Delete       ^KY││
│                                     │ Move         ^KV││
│                                     │ Mark End     ^KK││
│                                     │ Mark Start   ^KB││
│                                     │ Read from file ^KR││
│                                     │ Write to file  ^KW││
│                                     └─────────────────┘│
│                                                        │
└────────────────────────────────────────────────────────┘
```

Figure 19.3: The Block Commands menu

Using the Cursor Controls

In addition to the Arrow keys, 1Word provides commands to quickly move around within large files. Table 19.3 shows the ones you will use most often.

Keys	Description
Ctrl-Left Arrow	Moves the cursor one word to the left.
Ctrl-Right Arrow	Moves the cursor one word to the right.
Home	Moves the cursor to the beginning of the line.
End	Moves the cursor to the end of the line.
Ctrl-Home	Moves the cursor to the top of the screen.

Table 19.3: 1Word cursor commands

Keys	Description
Ctrl-End	Moves the cursor to the bottom of the screen.
Page Up	Moves the cursor to the previous screen of text.
Page Down	Moves the cursor to the next screen of text.
Ctrl-Page Up	Moves the cursor to the beginning of the file.
Ctrl-Page Down	Moves the cursor to the end of the file.

Table 19.3: 1Word cursor commands (continued)

Using the File Commands

When you have finished your list, you may want to print it, and you will definitely want to save it. These operations are available on the File commands menu.

1. Press Ctrl-U to display the 1Word menu. Now highlight *File* and press Enter. The File commands menu appears.

2. To print the list, highlight *Print using PRN,* and press Enter.

3. Accept the default lines per page number shown, or press Backspace to delete it, then type another number. Then press Enter. Your document will be printed.

4. Now let's save the file. Press Ctrl-U to display the 1Word menu. *File* is still highlighted, since it was the last item you selected, so just press Enter. Now highlight *save and Continue,* and press Enter. The document will be saved, and you can continue editing if you wish.

From the File commands menu you can:

- Quit without saving.
- Save the current file and exit.
- Save the current file and continue editing it.
- Save the current file under another name.
- Save the current file and begin editing another file.
- Print the current file.
- Import another file.
- Write a marked block.

When commands are displayed on menus, their accelerator keys are shown on the right. As you become familiar with the commands, you may want to use these keys instead of the menus. Remember, you can always see a list of 1Word's commands and keys by pressing F1 or selecting Help from the menu.

Quitting 1Word

To quit 1Word, select the save and/or exit option of your choice from the File commands menu. Or press Esc to display the Quit commands menu and select from the commands shown.

Step 20

Customizing XTreeGold

⏱ 15

XTreeGold lets you customize many program features and configure options to suit your preferences and work style. This step shows you how to use the Configuration utility to customize XTreeGold. The configuration options are slightly different in versions 1.0 and 2.0, but most of the capabilities described here are available to 1.0 users.

The Configuration Utility

XTreeGold's configuration utility lets you define precisely how you want many program areas to operate. It also lets you change the display on a color or monochrome monitor. You can run the configuration utility from within XTreeGold or from the DOS prompt.

Select the *Configuration* command from the XTree pull-down menu, or select *configure* from the Alt directory command menu. Any of these methods will work.

Configuring from within XTreeGold

- Open the XTree pull-down menu and click the left mouse button on *Configuration* or press C.
- Double-click *DIR COMMANDS*, then click *configure* in the command menu.
- Press Alt-F10.

Configuring from outside XTreeGold

To run the configuration utility from outside XTreeGold, at the DOS prompt type

    XTG_CFG

Then press Enter.

When you run the configuration utility from outside XTreeGold, all the options become available. A few options, including the Security options, cannot be changed from within XTreeGold.

Whether you begin the utility from inside or outside XTreeGold, the first thing you will see is the Configuration main menu (Figure 20.1).

From this menu, you can:

- Scroll through all the configuration screens and select items you would like to change.
- Change the way colors are displayed.
- Undo the changes you have made, and restore the permanent configuration settings from disk.
- Undo the changes you have made and restore the original factory default settings from disk.
- Save the changes you have made and exit back to XTreeGold.

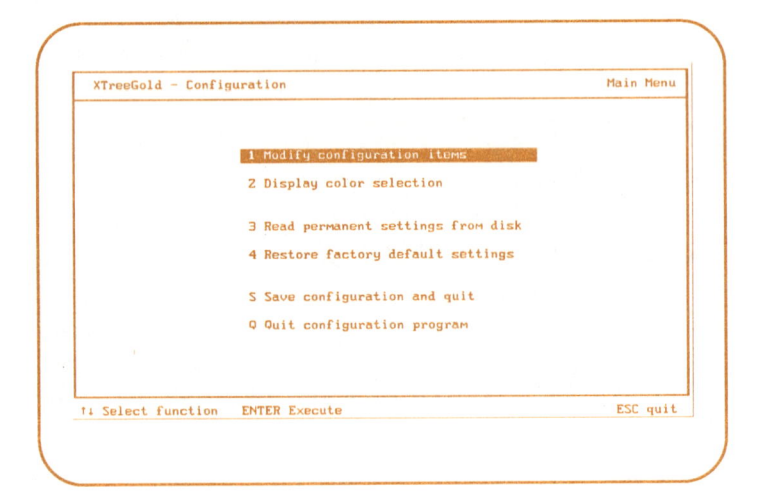

```
XTreeGold - Configuration                              Main Menu


                1 Modify configuration items

                2 Display color selection

                3 Read permanent settings from disk

                4 Restore factory default settings

                5 Save configuration and quit

                Q Quit configuration program



   ↑↓ Select function   ENTER Execute                   ESC quit
```

Figure 20.1: The Configuration main menu

- Exit back to XTreeGold without saving the changes you have made.

To select any item from a configuration window:

- Highlight the item with the left mouse button.
- Press the highlighted number or letter at the left of each item.
- Press the Up or Down Arrow to highlight the item.

To move from window to window, use the same techniques to select Next page, Previous page or Main menu.

The mouse works only within the box on the screen. You cannot use the mouse to select items at the bottom of the screen, such as the words *ESC quit* or *ESC Return to main menu*.

To change an item, first select the item, using the left mouse button, Arrow keys, or highlighted number or letter. Then, use one of the following techniques.

- Click the left mouse button.
- Press the highlighted number or letter to the left again.
- Press Enter.

Although it's probably quicker to use the same technique, for example, pointing and clicking with the mouse or pressing the highlighted number or letter twice, you can combine the techniques that you find easiest to use.

XTreeGold has five pages of configuration options, divided into the categories shown in Table 20.1.

Selecting items in configuration windows

Changing an item

Configuration options

Category	Description
Application Menu	Choose whether or not the Application menu is displayed immediately when you start XTreeGold, and whether you will return to XTreeGold immediately after selecting a menu item.
Directories	Indicate storage location of the XTreeGold program files and an alternative text editing program.
Disk logging	Choose one of three logging methods as the default.
Display	Change the monitor type settings to improve the quality of the display.
File Window	Change the defaults for how items are displayed in the File windows.
File and Tree Windows	Change the directory and file names from upper case to lower case and change the mouse scroll bar.
International	Change date, time and numeric formats as needed.
Memory Utilization	Indicate how application programs, the mouse, and the text editor should use memory.
Miscellaneous	Select how you want to handle some confirmation prompts and error messages, and the archive attribute on copied files.
Mouse	Change the mouse acceleration.
Printer	Modify the standard printer configuration items.

Table 20.1: Configuration option categories

Category	Description
Security	Indicate whether to allow changes in hex mode to the application menu or files. Indicate whether system and hidden files and directories will be displayed.
Tree Window	Change the defaults for how items are displayed in the Directory window.

Table 20.1: Configuration option categories (continued)

As you scroll through the configuration options, a single-line summary of each option appears in turn at the bottom of the screen. This is the only "help" available while using the configuration utility. You cannot press F1 for help until you exit back to XTreeGold.

Configuration help

Modifying Configuration Options

To modify a configuration item, simply select the first option on the main menu and then select each item you want to change. For example, here are the steps you would follow to eliminate the confirmation prompt for *Quitting XTreeGold* and to automatically run your own text editor or word processing program when you select the *Edit* command. We will start from XTreeGold.

1. Press Alt-F10 or open the XTree pull-down menu and click the left mouse button on *Configuration*.

2. The first item is highlighted on the main menu. Press Enter or click on *Modify configuration items*.

3. Press 4, or click on *Editor program:* or select it with the Down Arrow to make a change in the default text editing program.

4. Press Enter or click on *Editor program:* to display the editing line.

5. At the prompt, type in the full path and file name to execute. For example, type **C:\WP51\WP.EXE** and press Enter.

6. Now, press N twice or double-click on *Next page* to move to page 3, where the memory utilization items are displayed.

7. Press 8 or click on *Text editor* or select it with the Down Arrow to make a change in the memory available for your editing program.

8. Press Enter or click on *Text editor* to change the memory from *available memory* to *all memory*. The *all memory* setting optimizes the performance of your text editor when you run the editor from XTreeGold.

9. Press N or click on *Next page* to move to page 5, where the miscellaneous items are displayed.

10. Press 5 or point to *Skip Quit command prompt* with the mouse or Down Arrow to select the item that will let you eliminate the confirmation prompt when you quit XTreeGold.

11. Press Enter, or click on *Skip Quit command prompt,* to change the *no* to *yes.*

12. To go back to the Configuration main menu, press M or click on *Main menu.*

13. From the Configuration main menu, press S or click on *Save configuration and quit.* At the prompt, press Y or click on *Yes.*

Your changes are saved and will be used by XTreeGold until you override them with other changes.

Modifying the Display Colors

XTreeGold's configuration utility lets you change the display colors, or, on a monochrome display, the shading for each of the

Customizing XTreeGold 135

following screen elements:

- Cursor bar.
- Highlight characters such as the hotkeys, the directory tree and file names.
- Lowlight characters such as the statistics boxes and command menus.
- Mouse cursor.

For all of these, you can change both the character color and the background color.

The mouse is inactive in the color configuration window, and no help screens are available until you return to XTreeGold.

To modify any of the screen colors:

1. Press Alt-F10 or open the XTree pull-down menu and click on *Configuration* to display the configuration main menu.

2. Highlight *2 Display color selection,* and click on it with the mouse or press Enter. The color configuration screen appears (Figure 20.2). From this screen, you can change the components on the Main Display, the File windows and/or the pull-down menus.

3. Press Tab twice to change the colors in the File windows. You will notice that the color bar moves so that it is under the File window simulator.

4. *Highlight characters* is the first item selected by default. Press F5 and F6 to scroll through the colors until you find the one you want for the highlight characters.

5. Now press F7 and F8 to scroll through the colors until you find the one you want for the characters' background. You may have to go back and forth between character and background colors until you find a combination you like.

136   *Up & Running with XTreeGold 2*

6. Now stay on the same screen and, by pressing L, change the colors for the lowlight characters. Use the F5, F6, F7 and F8 keys until you find a combination you like.

7. Change the Cursor bar colors by pressing C, then using the function keys as stated in #6.

8. Finally, change the Mouse cursor colors by pressing M, then using the function keys as stated in #6.

9. Once you have changed all the colors for the File windows, press Tab to move to the Main Display, and repeat the process.

10. On version 2.0, you can repeat the process again to change the colors on the pull-down menus.

11. Once you have finished all your color changes, press Esc to return to the configuration main menu.

12. From this main menu, press S or click on *Save configuration and quit*. At the prompt, press Y or click *Yes*.

Your new color selections are displayed immediately.

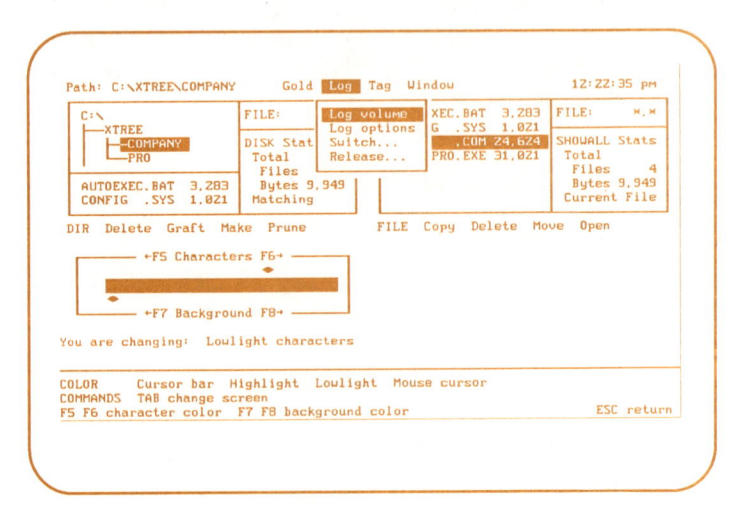

Figure 20.2: The color configuration screen

Index

A

across drives option (Compare), 113
Add command, 85
Add item command, 86
All disk files command, 23
All in window command, 20–21, 24
all option (Compare), 113
Alt menu, 12–13
appending file data, 71
Application menu
    collapsing and expanding, 89
    configuration option for, 132
    creating, 2–4, 83–85
    modifying, 84–88
    organizing, 88–89
Application Scanner, 3–4
applications, launching, 91–94
Arc File window, 102–103
Arc format
    archiving files in, 95–99
    extracting files from, 101–106
archiving files, 95–99, 101–106
arrow keys
    with Autoview window, 66
    with command history, 14–15
    with file and directory selection, 8
    with menu commands, 12–13
    with 1Word, 124–126
    with prompt responses, 14
asterisks (*)
    for branch quick logging, 34–35
    in file specifications, 17
    in searches, 79
Autoview window, 65–67

B

Backspace key, 14, 125
backups, compressing files for, 95–99
batch files
    for application launching, 91–93
    for scripts, 87–88
    for starting, 2–3, 5
Block menu item (1Word), 123, 126
Bookmark menu (View), 74
boxes, 7
Branch File window, 8–9
branches
    comparing, 112
    copying, 41–43
    deleting, 50–51
    logging, 26, 28, 30
    moving, 58–60
    quick logging of, 34
    searching through, 79
browsing files, 65–69, 71–77, 104

C

case sensitivity in searches, 79, 122
collapsing
   Application menus, 89
   tree displays, 32–33
color, configuration of, 129, 134–136
command line, partial logging from, 27
command menus, 11–12
comparing files, 107–108
   between directories, 111–112
   in directories, 109–111
   between volumes, 113–114
Compatibility option (archiving), 97
complete logs, 25–26
compressing files, 95–99
configuration utility, 129–136
conflicting files in Undelete window, 116–118
copying files, 37
   branches, 41–43
   directories, 40–41
   individual, 38–39
   parts of, 76–77
   volumes, 44
   in windows, 39–40
Create easy access batch file command, 3
Ctrl menu, 12–13, 18
cursor controls with 1Word, 126–127
customizing XTreeGold, 129–136

D

data files for application launching, 91
database files, 71, 74–76
date with 1Word, 121
default file specifications, 17
default prompt responses, 14
Delete key, 14, 125
Delete menu item (1Word), 123
deleting
   Application menu items, 85
   directories, 48–51
   disk contents, 51–52
   files, 45–48, 50–51
   menu items, 123
Destination directory window, 15
diamonds for tagged files, 18
DIR COMMANDS, 12–13
directories
   comparing files between, 111–112
   comparing files in, 109–111
   copying, 40–41
   deleting, 48–51
   deleting files in, 47–48
   displaying, 7, 26–27, 31–35, 133
   for installation, 3, 132
   listing, 8
   moving, 53–54, 59–60
   moving files in, 56–57
   quick logging, 33–34
   renaming, 63
   searching through, 79
   selecting files in, 20–23

Index

Directory menu, 11
Directory window, 7, 9, 97
Disk specification box, 10
disks
   deleting contents of, 51–52
   for installation, 3
   logging, 25–28, 132
   releasing, from memory, 29–30
   searching through, 79–81
   selecting files on, 23
   switching, 30
   for viewers, 4
Display option (Configuration), 132
displaying file contents, 4–5, 71–77, 105
DOS requirements, 1
dots (.) in directory trees, 32
duplicate files, finding, 107–113

E

easy access batch files, 3, 5
Edit menus, 74, 84
editing. *See also* 1Word text editor
   files, 71, 92–93
   menu items, 84, 86-n-87
   prompt responses, 14
ellipses (...), 14
Encryption option (archiving), 97
End key, 8, 14, 126–127
entering text, 124–126
Exit command (Undelete), 117
Expanded File window, 8–9

expanding
   Application menus, 89
   tree displays, 32–33
extracting archived files, 101–106

F

fields, database, 75–76
File and Tree Windows option (Configuration), 132
FILE COMMANDS, 12–13
File menus, 11, 104, 123
File specification box, 10
File specification command, 17
File windows, 7–9, 132
files
   for application launching, 91–93
   archiving, 95–99
   comparing, 107–114
   conflicting, 116–118
   copying, 37–44, 76–77
   database, 71, 74–76
   deleting, 45–48, 50–51
   editing, 71, 92–93
   extracting, 101–106
   formats for, 68, 74–75
   moving, 53–60
   recovering, 115–118
   renaming, 61–63, 92
   for scripts, 87–88
   searching, 67, 69, 71, 74, 79–81
   selecting, 8, 17–24, 66–67
   spreadsheet, 71, 74–76
   for starting, 2–3, 5

tagging. *See* tagging files
viewing, 2, 4–5, 71–77, 105
word processing, 71, 74–75
Files in branch option (Release), 30
formats, file, 68, 74–75
formulas, spreadsheet, 75
full paths option (Copy with paths), 42

G

gathering file data, 71, 74, 76–77
Global File window, 8–9
goto bookmark commands, 74
Graft command, 53–54, 59–60
groups of files. *See* tagging files

H

hard disk space requirements, 1
Help command (Undelete), 117
Help menu item (1Word), 123
hex editing, 71
highlight bar, 8, 17
history, command, 14–15
Home key, 8, 14, 126
hotkeys, 13

I

Identical dates option (Compare), 109
Identical option (Compare), 108
individual files
copying, 38–39

deleting, 45–46
moving, 54–55
renaming, 61–62
selecting, 19–20, 24
Insert key, 14, 125
INSTALL program, 1
installation, 1–6
International option (Configuration), 132

K

keyboard for menu selection, 12–13

L

launching applications, 91–94
levels, logging, 26–28
listing files and directories, 8. *See also* tree display
logging
and directory trees, 31–32
and disk switching, 30
disks, 25–28
quick logging, 33–35
releasing of, 29–30

M

main display, 7, 10
marking files. *See* tagging files
matching paths option (Compare), 113
memory
configuration option for, 132

Index

logging disk and volumes into, 25–28
releasing disks and volumes from, 29–30
requirements for, 1
menu command, 83
Menu item (1Word), 123
menus, 10–12, 122–124. *See also* Application menu
Method option (archiving), 97
minus key (–) for quick logging, 34–35
Miscellaneous option (Configuration), 132
Modify configuration items command, 133
mouse, 8, 12–13, 132
moving
   Application menu items, 85
   directories, 53–54, 59–60
   files, 53–60

N

names
   for Application menu items, 85
   for directories, 63
   for files, 61–63, 92
   for volumes, 63–64
Newer option (Compare), 108
Newest date option (Compare), 109
Next disk command, 30
Next tagged file command, 73–74

O

Older option (Compare), 108
Oldest date option (Compare), 109
One level option (Log), 26, 28
1Word text editor, 119
   for batch files, 92–93
   commands for, 127–128
   cursor controls for, 126–127
   entering and editing text with, 124–126
   menus for, 122–124
   status box for, 120–122
Oops! command, 115–118
Opening
   applications, 91, 94
   archived files, 101–102
Options menus, 84, 123

P

Page Up and Page Down keys, 8, 127
parameters for batch files, 92
partial branch paths option (Copy with paths), 42–43
partial logs, 26–28
passwords for archived files, 95, 97, 106
Path identification line, 10
paths with 1Word, 120
Paths option (archiving), 97
plus sign (+)
   in Application menus, 88–89
   for branch quick logging, 34

in directory trees, 32
printing
   archived files, 104
   configuration option for, 132
   with 1Word, 127–128
prompts, responding to, 13–14
Prune command, 45, 49–51
pull-down menus, 10–12. *See also* Application menu

Q

question marks (?)
   and deleted files, 116
   in file specifications, 17
   in searches, 79
quick logging, 33–35
Quit command, 5–6

R

recovering deleted files, 115–118
Refresh directory option (Log), 27
releasing
   branches, 34–35
   disks and volumes, 29–30
Relog directory option (Log), 27
renaming
   Application menu items, 85
   directories, 63
   files, 61–63
   volumes, 63–64
restoring
   deleted files, 115–118
   tree structures, 33

S

saving
   commands, 14–15
   configuration changes, 130–131
   with 1Word, 127–128
Scope option (Compare), 109, 113
scripts, Application menu, 85–88
scrolling, 67, 73
searching
   files, 67, 69, 71, 74, 79–81
   with 1Word, 121–123
Security option (Configuration), 129, 133
selecting
   commands, 12–15
   directories, 8
   files, 8, 17–24, 66–67
   viewers, 4–5
   windows, 9
set bookmark commands, 74
shortcuts for command selection, 14–15
Showall command, 40, 47, 56
Showall File window, 8–9
Skip file command, 39
Small File window, 8–9
Sort criteria command (Undelete), 117
Speed/size option (archiving), 97
spreadsheet files, 71, 74–76
Standard menu, 12–13
starting XTreeGold, 5
Statistics box, 10, 116

Index 143

status box for 1Word, 120–122
Structure command, 76
subdirectories. *See* directories
switching logged disks, 30
symbols for tree displays, 31–32

T

tabs with 1Word, 121
Tag and Tagged menus, 11, 18, 67, 104
tagging files, 18–20
   for compression, 96
   for copying, 37, 39–43
   for deletion, 46–47
   in directories, 20–23
   on disks, 23
   for extraction, 106
   for moving, 56–57
   for renaming, 62–63
   for searching, 69, 79
   for viewing, 72–74
   in windows, 24
text editor. *See* 1Word text editor
text strings, searching for, 79–81
time with 1Word, 120, 123
tree display, 7
   configuration option for, 133
   customizing, 31–35
   logging, 26–27

U

Undelete window, 115–116
undeleting files, 115–118
Unique option (Compare), 108
Unique name option (Compare), 108

Untag command, 19–23
updating archived files, 97–99
user interface, 7–15

V

variables for batch files, 92
versions, replacing, 3
View menus, 67, 74
View window, 71–74
viewing files, 65–69, 71–77, 104
Volume menus, 11, 104
volumes
   comparing files between, 113–114
   copying, 44
   copying between, 42
   logging, 25–28
   moving files to, 58–59
   releasing, from memory, 29–30
   renaming, 63–64
   searching through, 80–81

W

Wash disk command, 115
wild cards
   in file specifications, 17
   with renaming files, 62–63
   in searches, 79–80
Window menus, 11, 104
windows, 7
   copying files in, 39–40
   deleting files in, 46–47
   moving files in, 56–57
   renaming files in, 62–63
   selecting, 9

tagging files in, 24
word processing files, 71, 74–75
word wrap with 1Word, 121

X

XTG_CFG command, 129
xtgold command, 5
XTree menus, 11, 67, 74, 84, 103–104

Z

Zip Directory window, 102
Zip format
  archiving files in, 95–99
  extracting files from, 101–106
zooming, 68

Selections from The SYBEX Library

UTILITIES

Mastering the Norton Utilities 5
Peter Dyson
400pp, Ref. 725-8

This complete guide to installing and using the Norton Utilities 5 is a must for beginning and experienced users alike. It offers a clear, detailed description of each utility, with options, uses and examples—so users can quickly identify the programs they need and put Norton right to work. Includes valuable coverage of the newest Norton enhancements.

Mastering PC Tools Deluxe 6
For Versions 5.5 and 6.0
425pp. Ref. 700-2

An up-to-date guide to the lifesaving utilities in PC Tools Deluxe version 6.0 from installation, to high-speed back-ups, data recovery, file encryption, desktop applications, and more. Includes detailed background on DOS and hardware such as floppies, hard disks, modems and fax cards.

Mastering SideKick Plus
Gene Weisskopf
394pp. Ref. 558-1

Employ all of Sidekick's powerful and expanded features with this hands-on guide to the popular utility. Features include comprehensive and detailed coverage of time management, note taking, outlining, auto dialing, DOS file management, math, and copy-and-paste functions.

Up & Running with Norton Utilities
Rainer Bartel
140pp. Ref. 659-6

Get up and running in the shortest possible time in just 20 lessons or "steps." Learn to restore disks and files, use UnErase, edit your floppy disks, retrieve lost data and more. Or use the book to evaluate the software before you purchase. Through Version 4.2.

Up & Running with PC Tools Deluxe 6
Thomas Holste
180pp. Ref.678-2

Learn to use this software program in just 20 basic steps. Readers get a quick, inexpensive introduction to using the Tools for disaster recovery, disk and file management, and more.

OPERATING SYSTEMS

The ABC's of DOS 4
Alan R. Miller
275pp. Ref. 583-2

This step-by-step introduction to using DOS 4 is written especially for beginners. Filled with simple examples, *The ABC's of DOS 4* covers the basics of hardware, software, disks, the system editor EDLIN, DOS commands, and more.

**ABC's of MS-DOS
(Second Edition)**
Alan R. Miller
233pp. Ref. 493-3

This handy guide to MS-DOS is all many PC users need to manage their computer files, organize floppy and hard disks, use EDLIN, and keep their computers organized. Additional information is given about utilities like Sidekick, and there is a DOS command and program summary. The second edition is fully updated for Version 3.3.

DOS Assembly Language Programming
Alan R. Miller
365pp. 487-9

This book covers PC-DOS through 3.3, and gives clear explanations of how to assemble, link, and debug 8086, 8088, 80286, and 80386 programs. The example assembly language routines are valuable for students and programmers alike.

DOS Instant Reference
SYBEX Prompter Series
Greg Harvey
Kay Yarborough Nelson
220pp. Ref. 477-1, 4 ¾" × 8"
A complete fingertip reference for fast, easy on-line help: command summaries, syntax, usage and error messages. Organized by function—system commands, file commands, disk management, directories, batch files, I/O, networking, programming, and more. Through Version 3.3.

Encyclopedia DOS
Judd Robbins
1030pp. Ref. 699-5
A comprehensive reference and user's guide to all versions of DOS through 4.0. Offers complete information on every DOS command, with all possible switches and parameters—plus examples of effective usage. An invaluable tool.

Essential OS/2
(Second Edition)
Judd Robbins
445pp. Ref. 609-X
Written by an OS/2 expert, this is the guide to the powerful new resources of the OS/2 operating system standard edition 1.1 with presentation manager. Robbins introduces the standard edition, and details multitasking under OS/2, and the range of commands for installing, starting up, configuring, and running applications. For Version 1.1 Standard Edition.

Essential PC-DOS
(Second Edition)
Myril Clement Shaw
Susan Soltis Shaw
332pp. Ref. 413-5
An authoritative guide to PC-DOS, including version 3.2. Designed to make experts out of beginners, it explores everything from disk management to batch file programming. Includes an 85-page command summary. Through Version 3.2.

Graphics Programming Under Windows
Brian Myers
Chris Doner
646pp. Ref. 448-8
Straightforward discussion, abundant examples, and a concise reference guide to graphics commands make this book a must for Windows programmers. Topics range from how Windows works to programming for business, animation, CAD, and desktop publishing. For Version 2.

Hard Disk Instant Reference
SYBEX Prompter Series
Judd Robbins
256pp. Ref. 587-5, 4 ¾" × 8"
Compact yet comprehensive, this pocket-sized reference presents the essential information on DOS commands used in managing directories and files, and in optimizing disk configuration. Includes a survey of third-party utility capabilities. Through DOS 4.0.

Inside DOS: A Programmer's Guide
Michael J. Young
490pp. Ref. 710-X
A collection of practical techniques (with source code listings) designed to help you take advantage of the rich resources intrinsic to MS-DOS machines. Designed for the experienced programmer with a basic understanding of C and 8086 assembly language, and DOS fundamentals.

Mastering DOS
(Second Edition)
Judd Robbins
722pp. Ref. 555-7
"The most useful DOS book." This seven-part, in-depth tutorial addresses the needs of users at all levels. Topics range from running applications, to managing files and directories, configuring the system, batch file programming, and techniques for system developers. Through Version 4.

MS-DOS Power User's Guide, Volume I
(Second Edition)
Jonathan Kamin
482pp. Ref. 473-9
A fully revised, expanded edition of our best-selling guide to high-performance DOS techniques and utilities—with details on Version 3.3. Configuration, I/O, directory structures, hard disks, RAM disks, batch file programming, the ANSI.SYS device driver, more. Through Version 3.3.

Understanding DOS 3.3
Judd Robbins
678pp. Ref. 648-0
This best selling, in-depth tutorial addresses the needs of users at all levels with many examples and hands-on exercises. Robbins discusses the fundamentals of DOS, then covers manipulating files and directories, using the DOS editor,

printing, communicating, and finishes with a full section on batch files.

Understanding Hard Disk Management on the PC
Jonathan Kamin
500pp. Ref. 561-1

This title is a key productivity tool for all hard disk users who want efficient, error-free file management and organization. Includes details on the best ways to conserve hard disk space when using several memory-guzzling programs. Through DOS 4.

Up & Running with Your Hard Disk
Klaus M Rubsam
140pp. Ref. 666-9

A far-sighted, compact introduction to hard disk installation and basic DOS use. Perfect for PC users who want the practical essentials in the shortest possible time. In 20 basic steps, learn to choose your hard disk, work with accessories, back up data, use DOS utilities to save time, and more.

Up & Running with Windows 286/386
Gabriele Wentges
132pp. Ref. 691-X

This handy 20-step overview gives PC users all the essentials of using Windows—whether for evaluating the software, or getting a fast start. Each self-contained lesson takes just 15 minutes to one hour to complete.

NETWORKS

The ABC's of Local Area Networks
Michael Dortch
212pp. Ref. 664-2

This jargon-free introduction to LANs is for current and prospective users who see general information, comparative options, a look at the future, and tips for effective LANs use today. With comparisons of Token-Ring, PC Network, Novell, and others.

The ABC's of Novell Netware
Jeff Woodward
282pp. Ref. 614-6

For users who are new to PC's or networks, this entry-level tutorial outlines each basic element and operation of Novell. The ABC's introduces computer hardware and software, DOS, network organization and security, and printing and communicating over the netware system.

Mastering Novell Netware
Cheryl C. Currid
Craig A. Gillett
500pp. Ref. 630-8

This book is a thorough guide for System Administrators to installing and operating a microcomputer network using Novell Netware. Mastering covers actually setting up a network from start to finish, design, administration, maintenance, and troubleshooting.

COMMUNICATIONS

Mastering Crosstalk XVI (Second Edition)
Peter W. Gofton
225pp. Ref. 642-1

Introducing the communications program Crosstalk XVI for the IBM PC. As well as providing extensive examples of command and script files for programming Crosstalk, this book includes a detailed description of how to use the program's more advanced features, such as windows, talking to mini or mainframe, customizing the keyboard and answering calls and background mode.

Mastering PROCOMM PLUS
Bob Campbell
400pp. Ref. 657-X

Learn all about communications and information retrieval as you master and use PROCOMM PLUS. Topics include choosing and using a modem; automatic dialing; using on-line services (featuring CompuServe) and more. Through Version 1.1b; also covers PROCOMM, the "shareware" version.

Mastering Serial Communications
Peter W. Gofton
289pp. Ref. 180-2

The software side of communications, with details on the IBM PC's serial programming, the XMODEM and Kermit protocols, non-ASCII data transfer, interrupt-level programming and more. Sample programs in C, assembly language and BASIC.